Careers in the
US Navy

Carla Mooney

© 2016 ReferencePoint Press, Inc.
Printed in the United States

For more information, contact:
ReferencePoint Press, Inc.
PO Box 27779
San Diego, CA 92198
www.ReferencePointPress.com

Picture Credits:
Cover: US Navy/Aviation Boatswain's Mate (Handling) Airman John Kelvin Chavez
  6: Accurate Art, Inc.
17: US Navy/Mass Communications Specialist 2nd Class Marcus L. Stanley
26: US Navy/Mass Communication Specialist 2nd Class Eric A. Pastor
54: US Navy/Mass Communication Specialist Seaman Apprentice Timothy Hale
66: US Navy/Mass Communication Specialist Seaman Raymond D. Diaz III

LIBRARY OF CONGRESS CATALOGING-IN-PUBLICATION DATA

Mooney, Carla, 1970– author.
    Careers in the US Navy / by Carla Mooney.
        pages cm. -- (Military careers)
    Includes bibliographical references and index.
    ISBN 978-1-60152-940-4 (hardback) -- ISBN 1-60152-940-6 (hardback) 1. United States. Navy--Vocational guidance. I. Title.
    VB259.M66   2016
    359.0023'73--dc23
                                                                                2015031312

Contents

Introduction: Launching Careers   4

Information Systems Technician   9

Culinary Specialist   16

Naval Aviator   24

Navy Diver   32

JAG Lawyer   39

Civil Engineer   45

Hospital Corpsman   52

Nuclear Surface Warfare Officer   59

Cryptologic Technician   65

Interview with a Navy Civil Engineer   73

Find Out More   75

Other Jobs in the Navy   76

Index   77

About the Author   80

Launching Careers

With 70 percent of the earth covered in water, 80 percent of the world's population living near coastal areas, and 90 percent of global commerce using the seas, the need for naval power is stronger than ever. Since its formation in 1775, the Navy has defended the seas and protected the United States, its citizens, and its allies. The Navy trains, maintains, and equips naval forces to fight and win wars, deter threats, and maintain freedom on the world's waters. From the sea and shore bases, the Navy defends the United States and its allies and protects the right to trade freely on the world's oceans.

The Navy primarily operates on the world's waterways. Navy ships, submarines, and aircraft patrol the world's oceans, canals, and rivers. On the job, navy personnel operate almost every type of military equipment, from aircraft carriers to nuclear submarines.

Many Opportunities

Many people are needed to keep the world's most dominant naval force operating smoothly. As of June 2015, the Navy employed nearly 440,000 active-duty and reserve personnel. Navy personnel operate, maintain, and repair nearly three hundred ships and thirty-seven hundred aircraft. They live and work on ships and submarines and serve on naval aircraft and at shore stations around the world. Each year, thousands of recruits join the Navy and fill new positions and jobs left open by service members who have returned to civilian life.

All types of people work for the Navy. There are hundreds of different navy career specialties that service members can pursue. The Navy employs engineers, doctors and nurses, information technology personnel, and chaplains. Navy personnel also work in mass communications, on flight operations teams, as human resource specialists, on construction battalions, and more. With so many opportunities, the Navy offers jobs that fit many backgrounds and interests.

Humanitarian Aid

In addition to defending the United States from sea-based threats, navy personnel often assist people and communities devastated by natural disasters. The men and women of the Navy provide humanitarian aid and disaster relief where and when it is needed. In 2010, for instance, a massive earthquake devastated Haiti, killing over 200,000 people, injuring 300,000, and leaving more than 1 million displaced. In response, the Navy sent over thirty ships to Haiti to provide medical care, fresh water, and shelter. A medical team of 550 navy doctors, nurses, and technicians provided care on the ground to the injured and homeless.

Commander Shelly Beck Benfield is the department head for internal medicine at the US Naval Hospital in Guam. She says that one of the highlights of her navy career was providing care for pediatric patients in Southeast Asia as part of Pacific Partnership 2010, an annual international humanitarian assistance project. As she explains on *Navy Medicine Live*, a blog sponsored by the Navy, "I served as the division officer of the inpatient pediatric unit where we cared for hundreds of pediatric patients in four different countries in Southeast Asia. Pacific Partnership certainly changes you as a person and a nurse. We changed the lives of so many children, providing care and surgeries they would not otherwise receive."

Requirements and Qualifications

To join the Navy, recruits must meet certain qualifications and commit to serve a certain amount of time. Candidates must have a high school diploma, be between the ages of seventeen and thirty-five, and pass a physical exam. Officers must have a bachelor's degree from an accredited college or university. They must be at least nineteen years old and no older than thirty-five, with some waivers available for positions in high-demand careers. In addition, recruits must be US citizens or have a green card and an established residence in the United States. While some combat positions, including navy diver, have been historically closed to women, the Navy has said it plans to open all positions to men and women by 2016.

US Armed Forces: Pay

In the US Armed Forces, pay for both enlisted personnel and officers depends on rank and years of service. Promotions depend on performance in addition to number of years served, with higher ranks translating to higher pay grades. The two graphs show monthly salaries commonly reached in the first four years of service.

Enlisted Pay

Monthly Salary Ranges for Enlisted Personnel with 0–4 Years in Service

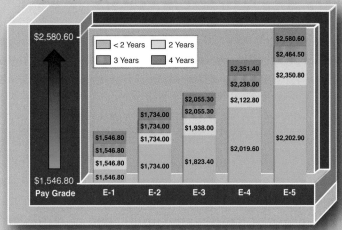

Officer Pay

Monthly Salary Ranges for Officers with 0–4 Years in Service

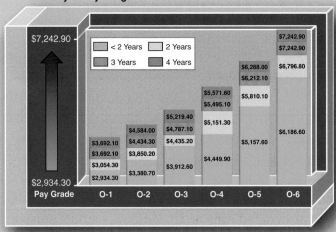

Note: Monthly salary ranges in both graphs are based on enlisted and officer pay scales effective January 1, 2015. The pay scales described here do not take into account the value of health benefits or housing and other allowances.

Source: Defense Finance and Accounting Service, "Military Pay Charts, 1949 to 2015," December 23, 2014. www.dfas.mil/militarymembers/payentitlements/military-pay-charts.html.

When enlisting in the Navy, recruits are screened to make sure they meet physical, academic, and moral standards. They are also tested for vocational aptitude, undergo background screening, and take an oath of enlistment. Candidates who do not meet the Navy's height, weight, or body fat requirements or do not pass a drug test or a criminal background check may be unable to enlist.

Enlisted vs. Officer Positions

Candidates are accepted into the Navy as either enlisted sailors or commissioned officers. The latter have a minimum of a four-year degree from a college or university and have completed officer training. The majority of navy service members are enlisted sailors. Enlisted sailors are the general workforce of the Navy, carrying out its daily operations. They are often highly specialized and perform many hands-on tasks. There are hundreds of positions in dozens of job areas, from cryptology to nuclear operations, available for enlisted sailors. Joining the Navy as either an enlisted sailor or an officer is a binding commitment. Becoming an enlisted sailor generally requires a service commitment of four years. Some positions with longer training periods may require longer service commitments. Enlisted sailors cannot quit until they have fulfilled their commitment.

Commissioned officers lead and manage enlisted personnel. There are many career options available for officers, from health care to aviation to engineering. Generally, officers are required to have a bachelor's degree or higher; however, highly trained technical specialists known as warrant officers are the exception and do not require a college degree. For officers, the service commitment is generally three to five years, with some positions requiring longer service commitments.

In the Navy, there are nine enlisted grades, five warrant officer ranks, and ten officer ranks. A service member's pay depends on his or her grade or rank and years of service. Promotion opportunities are available and are based on performance. Enlisted sailors who earn a bachelor's degree are eligible to be promoted to commissioned officers.

Type of Duty: Active vs. Reserve

When joining the Navy, recruits can choose to enter active duty, where they serve as full-time navy service members. Alternately, they may choose to join the Navy Reserves and serve on a part-time basis. Navy reservists train one weekend per month and two full weeks per year while working in a civilian career. When needed, reservists may be called up to active duty. In the three years after the 9/11 terrorist attacks in New York; Washington, DC; and Pennsylvania, nearly twenty-three thousand navy reservists were called up to serve on active duty around the world. They were sent to the Persian Gulf, the Pacific, and various US bases.

See the World

A career in the Navy is not a good fit for everyone. As with all branches of the military, service members are expected to follow rules and obey orders. Yet for many people, a navy career is very rewarding. Navy personnel can be found all over the world, in places as widespread as Egypt, Hong Kong, Brazil, Russia, and Australia. Many feel like Benfield, who says,

> When I graduated from nursing school, I had a strong desire to do something different than what my fellow nursing students were doing after graduation. I saw a flyer on my nursing school campus about Navy nursing and I was instantly intrigued. It immediately felt like a calling and I contacted the recruiter that very same day. At that time the motto was, "Join the Navy, See the world." And I have.

Information Systems Technician

Information technology (IT) plays an important role throughout the Navy's highly sophisticated networks and systems. The Navy uses computers to store and process data as well as to operate equipment during combat and peacetime. From ensuring everyday communications to safeguarding top secret information, information systems technicians (ISTs) are vital to ensuring that naval technology operates smoothly. These service members keep computer networks running properly and ensure the safety of sensitive data. As more sophisticated technology emerges in the future, the need for skilled ISTs will become even more critical.

ISTs have a broad range of responsibilities. They operate and maintain everything from electronic mail systems to shipboard control systems. As computer network administrators,

At a Glance:

Information Systems Technician

Minimum Educational Requirements
High school diploma or equivalent

Personal Qualities
Ability to work on a team and perform well under stress; good problem-solving skills

Certification and Licensing
Top secret/sensitive compartmented information security clearances

Working Conditions
On ships or submarines or at land-based communications stations in the United States or overseas

Salary Range
Monthly salary depends on pay grade and years of service

Future Job Outlook
Good

ISTs analyze, design, test, and evaluate network systems, Internet, intranet, and other data communications systems. They install new hardware and software programs, perform system backups, and maintain user accounts. Across the Navy's fleet of ships and aircraft carriers, they help set up computer systems. ISTs also work to defend the Navy's networks and computer systems from cyberattacks.

In addition, ISTs serve as a technology resource for other service members. They provide technical assistance to computer system users, answer questions, and fix computer problems. They also assist service members with the use of computer hardware and software, including printing, installing programs, and using operating systems.

ISTs also operate and maintain the Navy's communications systems, including its global satellite telecommunications systems. They make sure that the voice, data, video, and image communications systems are operating properly so that personnel get the information they need, when they need it.

ISTs are an important part of the Navy's Information Dominance Corps (IDC). Created in 2009, this group is made up of enlisted sailors, officers, and civilian professionals who specialize in information-intensive fields such as information technology, cryptology, and intelligence. Together, they work to develop and defend the Navy's intelligence, networks, and systems and to ensure technological superiority.

In a typical day, ISTs install, configure, and monitor the Navy's computer networks, hardware, and software. They perform preventive and corrective maintenance on state-of-the-art equipment. They write programs to handle data from a variety of applications. They answer questions and provide training and assistance to other service members. In addition, they implement computer and network security procedures and administer navy websites. Petty Officer First Class Israel Gomez, an information systems technician on a submarine, explains what his job is like in a video on the Navy's YouTube channel:

> As an information systems technician, you got to make
> sure that all your equipment is running 24/7. You got
> to make sure that your commanding officer can check
> his data, his e-mails. Make sure that your communi-

cations circuits are running so you can download and broadcast all your information no matter where you are. Navy is global. We have the largest Navy in the world so we got to make sure that we can communicate with any part of our Navy 24/7.

How Do You Become an Information Systems Technician?

Education

ISTs are enlisted sailors. As such, they are required to have a high school diploma. To prepare for this career, high school students should take classes in computer and network technology, computer programming, and math. Upon joining the Navy, all enlisted recruits complete an initial seven- to nine-week basic training, called recruit training or boot camp. Recruit training includes instruction in navy skills and protocols. It includes weapons training, team building, and strenuous physical exercise to improve a recruit's strength and endurance.

After recruit training, recruits receive specific training at "A" School at the Center for Information Dominance in Pensacola, Florida, to prepare them for careers as navy ISTs. This training lasts for twenty-four weeks and develops the working knowledge the sailors will need for their first assignments on a ship or at a shore station. Training includes classroom lectures as well as hands-on instruction with equipment. It includes extensive technical preparation in hardware and software operation, database design, computer networking, communications and operational systems, and security policies and procedures.

After this schooling, ISTs receive further experience and training on the job. They are eligible to take specialized operational and technical training courses. Because navy ISTs are responsible for computer and communications networks around the world, they also receive training with radio frequencies and satellite communications equipment.

Certification and Licensing

No special certification or licensing is required to be an IST. Nonetheless, because ISTs handle classified information and communications, they must have top secret/sensitive compartmented information security clearances. In order to gain these security clearances, a candidate must be a US citizen and not have a police record. He or she must also pass a background investigation, followed by a reinvestigation every five years. The candidate's immediate family members, including parents, siblings, and spouse, must also be US citizens.

Although the Navy does not require ISTs to hold special licenses or certifications, certifications are important to computer-related careers. There are many navy-funded certifications available for ISTs, including the Computing Technology Industry Association's A+, Linux+, and Server+ certifications; the Electronics Technicians Association's fiber optics installer and technician certifications; and the information security manager and security certified network specialist, professional, and architect certifications. In addition, the specialized training that navy ISTs receive can help them obtain civilian certifications from a number of national boards and organizations.

Volunteer Work and Internships

Students interested in a career as an IST can learn about navy life by participating in the Junior Reserve Officers' Training Corps (JROTC) in high school. Participation in the JROTC prepares students physically for basic training. JROTC members also participate in military drills and visit military bases to learn more about life in the armed services.

In addition, students can learn more about an information systems career by interning in a civilian company's information systems department or by shadowing an adult who has a job in this field. Companies in a variety of industries utilize technology and computer systems and employ professionals to maintain and operate these systems.

Physical Requirements, Skills, and Personality

To become an IST, candidates must meet the Navy's standards for physical fitness, weight, and/or percentage of body fat. They must also have normal color perception and hearing and no speech impediments.

ISTs should enjoy working with and have a good understanding of computers, electrical and mechanical systems, satellite systems, and other high-tech equipment. The work they perform involves mental analysis and problem solving, skills used when figuring out why systems are not working and quickly repairing them. ISTs should have the ability to understand and apply math concepts. They should also be able to speak and write well and communicate effectively. Other important skills for this career include the ability to perform detailed work and keep accurate records.

ISTs often work as part of a team. Therefore, the ability to work well with others is an important trait for people considering this career. Also, ISTs should be able to take and follow orders from superior officers. When stress levels are high during a military operation, ISTs should have the ability to operate calmly and efficiently.

On the Job

Working Conditions

ISTs can work on ships or submarines or at shore stations in the United States or overseas. Their work stations are generally located in clean, air-conditioned electronic equipment or computer rooms.

Life aboard a ship or submarine can take some getting used to. Deployments can last anywhere from a few weeks to several months. Although there are occasional stops at ports, navy personnel on sea tours spend most of their hours, days, and weeks at sea. While on a sea tour, the ship or submarine becomes the sailor's home away from home. Each sailor is assigned to a berthing area, which includes a storage locker and a sleeping rack. There are specific areas for eating, exercising, and recreation. Work schedules vary by ship or sub, but sailors typically work in shifts so that someone is on duty around the clock.

Earnings

In the Navy, basic pay is based on a service member's rank, also known as rate for enlisted personnel, and years of service. As of

January 1, 2015, the base salary for active-duty enlisted service members ranged from $18,564 to $91,020, according to the Navy CyberSpace website. In addition to basic pay, service members may qualify for extra pay or bonuses based on their job assignment or qualifications. For example, they can receive additional pay for foreign, hazardous, or submarine duty.

In addition, service members receive other benefits, which can amount to thousands of dollars. These benefits include paid vacation, housing and food allowances, and tax-free shopping privileges at military stores. Other benefits include comprehensive medical and dental care, education benefits, retirement benefits, and life insurance.

The Navy also offers enlistment bonuses, which depend on the terms of enlistment, military career choice, and the enlistee's education and qualifications. Enlistment bonuses range from about $2,000 to $40,000. Reenlistment bonuses are also available for service members in high-demand careers. As of July 2015, information systems technicians are eligible for reenlistment bonuses up to $75,000.

Opportunities for Advancement

The Navy provides service members with many opportunities for advancement. Service members typically receive a raise in pay each time they advance in grade or rank. Sailors generally enlist in the Navy in pay grade E-1, or seaman recruit. They may advance as high as E-9, master chief petty officer. The information systems technician field has its own career path to E-9, master chief information systems technician. As ISTs advance to E-7 and higher ranks, they take on more supervisory and administrative roles.

Promotion for enlisted service members depends on several factors, including performance evaluation marks and proficiency exam scores. Enlisted service members receive regular performance evaluations and must receive a minimum score to be eligible for a promotion. In addition, enlisted sailors from pay grade E-3 to E-6 must do well on promotion exams in order to earn a promotion to a higher rank. These examinations test the sailor for general navy knowledge and career-specific proficiency. Sailors who demonstrate a record of excellent performance and effective leadership are more likely to be promoted, along with those who earn civilian computer certifications.

The Navy also offers several paths for enlisted members who wish to be commissioned as navy officers. Enlisted members who have already earned a bachelor's degree in college can apply for Officer Candidate School. If they do not have a degree, the Navy offers enlisted members the opportunity to attend college full time and earn a bachelor's degree and then receive a commission. ISTs who complete navy training in information systems may be eligible to earn college credit hours toward a bachelor's or associate degree through the American Council on Education. A promotion to commissioned officer often results in a significant pay raise.

What Is the Future Outlook for Information Systems Technicians?

The United States currently spends a significant amount of its overall budget on national defense. The total number of active-duty and reserve personnel in the Navy is expected to remain about the same for the next several years. As ISTs leave the Navy or move on to other military careers, the Navy will need to fill these positions. As a result, new recruits for this field are constantly needed. In addition, as new global conflicts and threats emerge, there may be an additional demand for military personnel, including ISTs.

What Are Employment Prospects in the Civilian World?

After leaving the military, ISTs are qualified to work in a wide range of careers. The civilian certifications they earn during their time in the Navy can help them find civilian employment after leaving the military. Their specialized training, expertise, and security clearance may allow them to work in jobs with the federal government, including jobs in intelligence and information technology management. In addition, they may work as civilians for a variety of companies as computer and information systems managers; computer systems analysts; database administrators; network and computer systems administrators; and radio, cellular, and network equipment installers and repairers.

Culinary Specialist

What Does a Culinary Specialist Do?

Every day around the world, thousands of meals are prepared in navy kitchens. The availability of quality food is important for the health and morale of service members on ships and on shore. Culinary specialists operate and manage dining facilities and living quarters for navy personnel. They work on every ship, submarine, and shore base in the Navy. They also prepare food for special events for admirals and senior government officials. Navy culinary specialists even run the White House kitchen, preparing meals for the president of the United States.

Culinary specialists have many responsibilities. They estimate the amount and type of food and supplies needed in the kitchens. They assist supply officers with ordering the necessary items. When the ordered items are delivered, they assist with quantity checks and quality inspections. In the kitchen, culinary specialists plan, prepare, and serve meals. They maintain

At a Glance:
Culinary Specialist

Minimum Educational Requirements
High school diploma or equivalent

Personal Qualities
Enjoy working with people and members of a team; ability to do detailed work and keep accurate records; strong arithmetic and verbal skills and creative ability

Certification and Licensing
None

Working Conditions
Kitchens, dining areas, and food service storerooms on ships, submarines, or shore bases

Salary Range
Monthly salary depends on pay grade and years of service

Number of Jobs
More than 7,000

Future Job Outlook
Good

A US Navy culinary specialist prepares lunch for sailors aboard the guided-missile destroyer USS Chung-Hoon. *Culinary specialists prepare menus, order food supplies, and cook—in some instances, for thousands of navy personnel daily.*

the kitchen and dining areas, food service equipment, and storerooms to ensure they are clean and sanitary. Culinary specialists keep detailed records and submit required reports for food service activities. These records include procurement, receipts, expenditure procedures, food distribution and food cost control, food service surveys, and other reports.

In a typical day, culinary specialists prepare and serve many meals to service members. They prepare standard cuts of meats with cleavers and knives. They cook steaks, chops, and roasts. They bake or fry chicken, turkey, and fish. They prepare gravies and sauces to accompany main and side dishes. They bake breads, cakes, pies, and pastries. When the food is prepared, culinary specialists serve it in navy dining halls, hospitals, field kitchens, or on ships and submarines. They also clean all food service equipment and spaces daily to make sure everything is sanitary.

Culinary Specialist First Class Marco A. Coll-Dimayo prepares meals for a three-hundred-man crew on a navy destroyer, the *Dewey*. Aboard the *Dewey*, he supervises twenty-eight sailors. In addition to cooking, Coll-Dimayo attends trainings, maintains the ship's mess area, conducts food and supply inventories, prepares food orders, and records all food consumed. To prepare for this career, Coll-Dimayo attended basic culinary training at a culinary school in Texas after joining the Navy and then took advanced culinary school classes at Kapi'olani Community College in Hawaii. In an article in the *Rockford (IL) Register Star*, he explains, "Mostly though, the training comes from time spent on the job with receptions, banquets and luncheons I've had to manage." He says that he has prepared meals for many important people, including the princess of Cambodia, numerous ambassadors, and Prince Harry of England. Coll-Dimayo says that a career as a navy culinary specialist is the perfect fit for him. "I have always loved to cook since I was a child," he says. "I can honestly say there are never two days the same. It becomes very busy and it takes a special type of person, but for me, it's the best job I could ask for."

How Do You Become a Culinary Specialist?

Education

Culinary specialists are enlisted sailors. As such, they are required to have a high school diploma. To prepare for this career, high school students should take classes in math, nutrition, and culinary arts. Upon joining the Navy, recruits complete an initial seven- to nine-week basic training called recruit training or boot camp. Recruit training includes instruction in navy skills and protocols. It includes weapons training, team building, and strenuous physical exercise to improve a recruit's strength and endurance.

After recruit training, recruits who wish to become culinary specialists travel to the Joint Culinary Center of Excellence at Fort Lee, Virginia, where they receive formal technical training at "A" School to prepare them for careers as navy culinary specialists. This training lasts for nine weeks and develops the skills and knowledge the sailors will need for their first assignments on a ship or submarine or at a shore station. Training includes classroom lectures and hands-on practice in food preparation; nutrition; standard and dietetic menus and recipes; bakery products; food and supply ordering; and proper storage of meats, poultry, and other perishable items.

After this schooling, culinary specialists receive further experience and training on the job. If they will be serving on a submarine, they attend the four-week training program at the Basic Enlisted Submarine School in Groton, Connecticut. Culinary specialists are also eligible to take advanced training courses.

Certification and Licensing

No special certification or licensing is required to be a navy culinary specialist. Nonetheless, sailors have the opportunity to obtain civilian certifications from a number of national boards and organizations. For instance, they may choose to become certified bakers (with the Retail Bakers of America) or certified culinary administrators (with the American Culinary Federation, Inc.). These certifications may require additional training, education, or experience.

Volunteer Work and Internships

Students interested in a career as a culinary specialist can learn about navy life by participating in the Junior Reserve Officers' Training Corps (JROTC) in high school. Participation in the JROTC prepares students physically for basic training. JROTC members also participate in military drills and visit military bases to learn more about life in the armed services.

In addition, students can learn more about a culinary specialist career by interning in a café, restaurant, or cafeteria or by shadowing an adult who has a job in the food service industry. Food service specialist internships may also be available in hotels, hospitals, manufacturing plants, schools, and other organizations that have dining facilities.

Physical Requirements, Skills, and Personality

To become a culinary specialist, candidates must meet the Navy's standards for physical fitness, weight, and/or percentage of body fat. Unlike some other navy jobs, normal color perception is not a requirement for culinary specialists. In addition, they are not required to be US citizens.

Culinary specialists should have a good understanding of nutrition and the culinary arts and should have some creative ability. General cooking skills are important, along with knife skills and being able to adapt recipes for large or small groups. They will be expected to juggle multiple tasks at a time and move quickly from task to task in the kitchen. Culinary specialists should enjoy performing detailed work and be able to keep accurate records. They also should have the ability to understand and use basic arithmetic skills. Because people in this career frequently interact with others, culinary specialists should also be able to speak and write well and communicate effectively.

Culinary specialists often work as part of a team. Therefore, the ability to work well with others is an important trait for people considering this career. Also, culinary specialists should be able to take and follow orders from superior officers.

On the Job

Working Conditions

Culinary specialists can work aboard a ship or submarine or at shore stations in the United States or overseas. They work in kitchens, dining areas, living quarters, and food service storerooms.

Aboard ships and submarines, working quarters can be cramped. On the submarine USS *Jefferson City*, for instance, a team of six culinary specialists operates the sub's galley around the clock. They routinely cook four meals in eighteen hours to feed the crew of 130 sailors. The sub's galley is a small space, measuring only 10 feet (3 m) by 14 feet (4.2 m). Inside, culinary specialists operate two convection ovens, a microwave oven, a deep fryer, twin soup pots, and an industrial-sized mixer. The remaining space holds a small sink, sanitizer, cabinets, and drawers. Although space is limited, the culinary specialists make almost all of the sub's food from scratch, even baking their own bread. They take pride in adding creative twists to navy recipes, finding ways to improve food flavor, and presenting attractive meals. In an article for *QSR* magazine, culinary specialist chief Brandon Ramos explained that the sub's galley would not run smoothly without careful attention to planning and organization. "We pride ourselves on being clean and organized," he says. "We keep it up on a day-to-day basis. These guys are accountable. They know if they don't make the effort, the others suffer. We've never run short, we've never had to portion control. We don't waste either. They do a phenomenal job."

Earnings

In the Navy, basic pay is based on a service member's rank, also known as rate for enlisted personnel, and years of service. As of January 1, 2015, the base salary for active-duty enlisted service members ranged from $18,564 to $91,020, according to the Navy CyberSpace website. In addition to basic pay, service members may qualify for extra pay or bonuses based on their job assignment or qualifications. For example, they can receive additional pay for foreign, hazardous, or submarine duty.

In addition, service members receive other benefits, which can amount to thousands of dollars. These benefits include paid vacation, housing and food allowances, and tax-free shopping privileges at military stores. Other benefits include comprehensive medical and dental care, education benefits, retirement benefits, and life insurance.

The Navy also offers enlistment bonuses, which depend on the terms of enlistment, military career choice, and the enlistee's education and qualifications. Enlistment bonuses range from about $2,000 to $40,000. Reenlistment bonuses are also available for service members in high-demand careers. As of 2015, culinary specialists may be eligible for reenlistment bonuses up to $30,000.

Opportunities for Advancement

The Navy provides service members with many opportunities for advancement. Typically, service members receive a raise in pay each time they advance in grade or rank. Sailors generally enlist in the Navy in pay grade E-1, or seaman recruit. They may advance as high as E-9, master chief petty officer.

Promotion for enlisted service members depends on several factors, including performance evaluation marks and proficiency exam scores. Sailors who demonstrate a record of excellent performance and effective leadership are more likely to be promoted. Additionally, earning civilian certifications can make naval service members eligible for promotions.

A typical career path for a navy culinary specialist begins as a cook working in a kitchen to prepare food and maintain a dining area under the supervision of an experienced chef. Specialists with several years of experience may be promoted to chef. Chefs plan and prepare food menus and recipes. They supervise and train kitchen staff in the preparation of food. They also order food and supplies. Experienced chefs may later be promoted to food service supervisors. In this role, they set food service standards, policies, and work priorities. They prepare reports on food service activities; create and monitor food service budgets; and determine personnel, equipment, and supply needs.

Culinary specialists may choose to participate in a civilian apprenticeship to improve their job skills while still on active duty. Through the US Military Apprenticeship Program, culinary specialists can apprentice in trades including baker, cook, and food service manager. Upon completing the apprenticeship program, the sailor receives a nationally recognized certificate of completion from the US Department of Labor. Earning this certificate can make naval service members eligible for promotions.

The Navy also offers several paths for enlisted members who wish to be commissioned as officers. Enlisted members who have already earned a bachelor's degree can apply for Officer Candidate School. If they do not have a degree, the Navy offers enlisted members the opportunity to attend college full time and earn a bachelor's degree and then receive a commission. In addition, culinary specialists who complete navy technical and operational training in the field of food, restaurant, and lodging may be eligible to earn college credit hours toward a bachelor's or associate degree through the American Council on Education. A promotion to commissioned officer often results in a significant pay raise.

What Is the Future Outlook for Culinary Specialists?

The United States currently spends a significant amount of its overall budget on national defense. The total number of active-duty and reserve personnel in the Navy is expected to remain about the same for the next several years. As culinary specialists leave the Navy or move on to other military careers, the Navy will need to fill these open positions. As a result, new recruits for this field are constantly needed. In addition, as new global conflicts and threats emerge, there may be an additional demand for military personnel, including culinary specialists.

What Are Employment Prospects in the Civilian World?

After leaving the military, culinary specialists are qualified to work in a wide range of careers. Their specialized training and expertise, along with the civilian certifications they earn, can help them find civilian employment after leaving the military. Culinary specialists work in jobs with the federal government, including jobs in food service and food inspection and as cooks or bakers. In addition, they may work as civilians for a wide range of companies as chefs and head cooks, food preparation and serving workers, food service managers and supervisors, and food preparation workers. According to the US Department of Labor's *Occupational Outlook Handbook*, job opportunities for food service managers are expected to remain steady through 2022, and the employment of cooks is expected to grow approximately 10 percent through 2022.

Naval Aviator

What Does a Naval Aviator Do?

Airplanes and helicopters are an important part of the Navy. Naval aviators, or pilots, transport troops and equipment, fly on combat missions, perform rescue operations, and fly surveillance missions. Naval aviators do everything from looking for downed pilots in the ocean to finding and tracking enemy submarines. They fly a variety of aircraft, from advanced fighter jets to support helicopters.

In a typical day, a naval aviator may attend a mission briefing that can last for hours. To prepare for the day's mission, the aviator studies flight plans, maps, and mission details. Missions may involve dropping bombs on enemy targets, engaging in air combat with enemy aircraft, delivering supplies and troops, or flying close to the ocean surface to search for underwater threats such as mines or enemy submarines. Naval aviators also fly on search-and-rescue missions and conduct enemy surveillance by collecting photographic intelligence.

Before taking off and after landing, aviators inspect their aircraft, making sure it is in top condition. During flight, they

At a Glance:

Naval Aviator

Minimum Educational Requirements
Bachelor's degree

Personal Qualities
Strong desire to fly, ability to stay calm in stressful situations, self-confidence and decisiveness, normal color vision

Certification and Licensing
None

Working Conditions
Aircraft cockpits, shore bases, and aircraft carriers

Salary Range
Monthly salary depends on pay grade and years of service

Future Job Outlook
Good

monitor engine instruments and adjust flight controls. They direct the aircraft using radar, sight, and other navigation methods. At the same time, they may engage in air combat, take surveillance photos and video, or track enemy positions.

Naval aviators have superior flight skills and concentration. They can land a high-performance jet on the deck of an aircraft carrier in the middle of the night in rolling seas. Flying a few feet above the ocean, they track submarines beneath the surface. They perform missions under pressure. In addition to flying, aviators perform key tasks in navigation, air traffic control, and flight operations.

Lieutenant Commander James Waddell is a navy pilot who has traveled the world in his job, landing in more than thirty countries. His missions vary from day to day, with no day being like another. Waddell has flown many aircraft in his navy career. On Today's Military, a website sponsored by the Department of Defense, he explains that the variety he finds in his job makes it exciting: "The beauty of naval aviation is that you never know where on the map it is going to take you."

How Do You Become a Naval Aviator?

Education

To prepare for a career as a naval aviator, high school students should take classes in physical education, math, computer science, physics, and engineering. College students can choose any major, although a technical field is preferred.

All naval aviators are commissioned officers and must have a minimum of a bachelor's degree from an accredited college or university. In addition, they must successfully complete officer's training. To become an officer, recruits can enroll in a Reserve Officers' Training Corps (ROTC) program at a civilian college. In this program, they will attend military classes and drills as well as report for midshipman assignments during the summers. Other candidates may choose to attend the US Naval Academy. Admission to the Naval Academy is highly competitive, with only about 10 percent of applicants being accepted each year. These students typically have impeccable academic records and leadership experience. Recruits who already have a

Naval aviators with the US Seventh Fleet assist in international search-and-rescue operations for a missing commercial airliner. Navy pilots transport troops and equipment, fly on combat missions, perform rescue operations, and fly surveillance missions.

bachelor's degree can attend Officer Candidate School, an intensive twelve-week course in military studies held at the naval air station at Newport, Rhode Island.

To become a naval aviator, candidates must score well on the Aviation Selection Test Battery. The Navy uses the test to select candidates for pilot and flight officer training programs. It consists of seven subtests: math skills, reading comprehension, mechanical comprehension, aviation and nautical information, naval aviation trait facet inventory, performance-based measures battery, and a biographical inventory.

Once an officer is commissioned, he or she attends aviation training. This training begins with Aviation Preflight Indoctrination, a six-week air course that involves the study of the fundamentals of aerodynamics, aviation weather, aircraft engines and systems, flight rules and regulations, air navigation, and water survival. Student naval aviators (SNAs) also learn about aviation physiology, or how flight affects the human body. Upon completing this course, SNAs attend primary flight training, a six-month introduction to flying. Primary training includes classes, along with simulator training and flight training. The training introduces the student aviators to the types of aircraft they might fly and how to operate basic flight instruments. They also learn precision aerobatics, formation flying, and night flying, and get experience operating radio instruments. After successfully completing primary training, SNAs move on to intermediate flight training and enter one of five pipelines based on their performance and navy needs. In this training, they learn more about navigation and air traffic control and take practice flights to other training bases. The final stage of navy flight school, advanced training, teaches mission-specific skills such as air-to-air combat, bombing, search and rescue, aircraft carrier qualifications, over-water navigation, and low-level flying. Upon completing advanced training, SNAs earn their wings of gold, or pilot insignia. Naval aviators then are assigned to aircraft-specific training for the type of plane they will fly on assignment.

Physical Requirements

In addition to being US citizens, naval aviators must be physically fit. It can take a lot of stamina to pilot an aircraft for hours at a time. Fighter pilots who fly at high speeds must be physically strong enough to withstand powerful g-forces, the force of Earth's gravity pulling down on an object. Aviators' vision can be no worse than 20/40 uncorrected and correctable to 20/20. They must also have normal color vision and no problems with depth perception. Officer candidates must be between nineteen and twenty-six years old at the time of commissioning. In some cases, candidates who have served on active duty can extend the maximum age to twenty-nine.

Candidates must also take an aviation physical exam to determine if they are medically able to fly. They must have good hearing, normal blood pressure and heart rate, and no physical handicaps that could interfere with their ability to fly. Quick reflexes, good eye-hand coordination, and good spatial perception are also needed.

Naval aviators must meet specific height and weight requirements.

Generally, a naval aviator must be at least 5 feet 2 inches (157 cm) tall and no taller than 6 feet 5 inches (196 cm). They must also weigh no less than 103 pounds (47 kg) or more than 245 pounds (111 kg). The Navy uses a method called anthropometrics to determine if the height and weight of a student aviator is safely compatible with navy aircraft. These measurements assess whether an aviator will fit in a plane's cockpit. They include a sitting height, buttock-to-knee length, thumb-tip reach, and stature. For example, the Navy uses sitting height to make sure the aviator's head will not hit the top of the cockpit and that he or she will be able to see clearly out of the cockpit. Although both men and women can become naval aviators, female aviators are currently not permitted to fly on direct-combat missions.

Skills and Personality

Successful naval aviators have several personal characteristics in common. They usually have a strong drive to achieve, self-discipline, and are conscientious. Pilots follow detailed flight plans and go through comprehensive checklists each time they fly. On each mission, they monitor multiple controls and instruments and supervise flight crew members while also performing mission tasks such as air combat or surveillance. As such, being detail oriented and able to handle several tasks at once are also good traits to have.

Because many things can go wrong during a mission, naval aviators should be able to think quickly on their feet, troubleshoot, and solve problems. They must be able to keep calm during times of intense pressure and stress and be able to make quick, logical decisions. In addition, as officers, naval aviators should have strong leadership skills. Officers are responsible for the safety and protection of their flight crew, and they serve as role models for enlisted navy service members.

Volunteer Work and Internships

Students interested in a career as a naval aviator can learn about navy life by participating in the Junior Reserve Officers' Training Corps (JROTC) in high school and the ROTC in college. Participation in the JROTC and ROTC prepares students physically for basic training. Members also participate in military drills and visit military bases to learn more about life in the armed services. College ROTC members have the opportunity to participate in summer training that often includes airborne training.

On the Job

Working Conditions

Naval aviators can be sent on missions or assignments anywhere around the world. They may work from naval carrier battle groups, sea-based platforms, naval air stations, or other shore locations. They take off and land on modern airfields, makeshift airstrips, or moving aircraft carriers. They fly in all types of weather and situations. In the air, naval aviators fly long hours in enclosed cockpit spaces and sometimes deal with the weight of gravity during certain turns and maneuvers. On the ground, naval aviators spend a lot of time in briefings and meetings about missions, sometimes waiting in a ready room to be called to duty. Other times, naval aviators perform maintenance and checkups on their aircraft to make sure the plane is ready for its next mission. Because missions can arise at any time, naval aviators are prepared to fly at any time, day or night.

Earnings

In the Navy, basic pay is based on a service member's rank and years of service. As of January 1, 2015, the base salary for active-duty officers ranged from $35,208 to $237,156, according to the Navy CyberSpace website. In addition to basic pay, service members may qualify for extra pay or bonuses based on their job assignment or qualifications. For example, they can receive additional pay for foreign, hazardous, or submarine duty. Many naval aviators generally receive an additional $125 per month in flight pay. Active-duty commissioned officers on aviation duty can also earn aviation career incentive pay, which ranges from $125 to $840 monthly, depending on years of service.

In addition, service members receive other benefits, which can amount to thousands of dollars. These benefits include paid vacation, housing and food allowances, and shopping privileges at military stores. Other benefits include comprehensive medical and dental care, education benefits, retirement benefits, and life insurance.

The Navy also offers enlistment bonuses, which depend on the terms of enlistment, military career choice, and the enlistee's education and qualifications. Enlistment bonuses range from about $2,000 to $40,000. Reenlistment bonuses are also available for service members in high-demand careers. Naval aviators who choose to reenlist after their initial enlistment can earn a bonus of up to $125,000.

Opportunities for Advancement

The Navy provides service members with many opportunities for advancement. Promotions are generally competitive and based on performance. Typically, service members receive a raise in pay each time they advance in grade. As naval aviators advance, they can be put in charge of several aircraft on a mission, command a squadron, or become a commander of an aircraft carrier.

What Is the Future Outlook for Naval Aviators?

The United States currently spends a significant amount of its overall budget on national defense. The total number of active-duty and reserve personnel in the Navy is expected to remain about the same for the next several years. As pilots leave the Navy or move on to other military careers, the Navy will need to fill these open positions. As a result, new recruits for this field are constantly needed. In addition, as new global conflicts and threats emerge, there may be an additional demand for military personnel, including naval aviators.

What Are Employment Prospects in the Civilian World?

With their navy flight training and experience, naval aviators are frequently able to obtain civilian certifications and licenses from national boards and organizations, such as a flight instructor license, commercial pilot license, or commercial helicopter license. Earning these certifications and licenses can help naval aviators find civilian employment after leaving the Navy.

After leaving the military, many navy pilots fly for commercial airlines or private companies. Some work for civilian companies as aerospace technicians and engineers, airfield operations specialists, aviation inspectors, air traffic controllers, flight engineers, aircraft maintenance, and transportation managers. According to the US Department of Labor's *Occupational Outlook Handbook*, job opportunities for commercial pilots are expected to increase approximately 9 percent through 2022. Opportunities for airline pilots, however, are expected to decline 7 percent as airlines try to increase profitability by reducing the number of flights flown and increasing passengers per flight.

Navy Diver

What Does a Navy Diver Do?

Navy divers perform a wide variety of underwater tasks, ranging from inspecting submarines to conducting salvage and recovery missions to participating in research projects. They dive in all sorts of conditions in oceans all around the globe. Some divers work at extreme depths for days or weeks at a time, and others work in freezing arctic waters. Regardless of where they work, navy divers are expected to accomplish tasks that few people have the skills to perform. In an article for the website Alert Diver Online, Chief Warrant Officer Coy Everage explains, "It's never dull. You could be placing explosives on a sunken object in a semi-permissive war-time environment during combat harbor clearance operations, or you could be scuba diving out of a small boat somewhere tropical, performing an environmental-impact study with other government agencies."

After they complete rigorous physical and academic training, navy divers can work on a variety of underwater projects. Using diving equipment, they locate and recover wreckage and downed aircraft on salvage and recovery missions.

At a Glance:
Navy Diver

Minimum Educational Requirements
High school diploma or equivalent

Personal Qualities
Excellent physical condition and swimming ability, comfortable in close spaces, good memory, ability to perform detailed tasks under pressure

Certification and Licensing
Security clearance

Working Conditions
Varies widely with water conditions around the world

Salary Range
Monthly salary depends on pay grade and years of service

Number of Jobs
Approximately 1,175

Future Job Outlook
Very good

They conduct submarine rescue operations and conduct harbor and waterway clearances. Navy divers also perform underwater repairs and maintenance and participate in construction and demolition projects. They perform jobs such as applying patches to ships and subs, clearing ship propellers, and underwater cutting and welding. They perform underwater work such as taking measurements, making templates and fittings, pouring cement, and removing and repairing ship parts such as rudders and propellers. They also use underwater demolitions to free submerged objects. Some navy divers work on underwater research projects. For example, divers with the Navy Experimental Diving Unit in Panama City, Florida, research and test-dive equipment, techniques, and medical treatments as well as study the physical and biological effects of diving on the human body.

As a navy diver, Iryll Jones performs underwater repairs on all types of vessels. On any day, he might be welding underwater on a submarine or repairing the hatchwork on a navy destroyer. He says that navy divers must be prepared for the unexpected as conditions can be demanding and change rapidly. In an article for the navy magazine *All Hands*, Jones explains that "the sea can be too rough or the water can be too cold." Jones has dived all over the world and adds that conditions and problems change depending on where the diver is. "Every environment is different," he says. "There's a million factors to consider." As chief petty officer, Jones supervises the diving team on his ship. He hands out daily assignments and makes sure that each diver is fit to dive that day. He also determines if ocean and weather conditions are safe for diving. "It's an enormous responsibility," says Jones. "Someone's life is depending on your decision."

How Do You Become a Navy Diver?

Education

Navy divers are enlisted sailors. As such, they are required to have a high school diploma. To prepare for this career, high school students should take classes in physics, marine sciences, engineering, and physical education. Upon joining the Navy, recruits complete an initial seven- to nine-week basic training, called recruit training or boot camp. Recruit training includes instruction in navy skills and protocols. It includes weapons training, team building, and strenuous physical exercise to improve a recruit's strength and endurance.

After recruit training, recruits who wish to become navy divers may apply for the navy challenge contract for divers at any time during their first enlistment. Candidates selected to move forward attend the Diver Preparation Course at the Naval Training Command in Great Lakes, Illinois. In this seven-week course, recruits take basic electrical and engineering courses along with water adaptability and physical fitness training.

After completing the Diver Preparation Course, candidates attend Second Class Dive School at the Naval Diving and Salvage Training Center in Panama City, Florida. In this fifteen-week course, they receive training in a variety of areas, including air and mixed-gas diving; diving medicine; dive planning and diving physics; underwater cutting and welding; demolition; recompression chamber operations; underwater hydraulic tools; and ship maintenance, repair, and salvage. After completing Second Class Dive School, recruits are assigned to one of the navy diver units, where additional training takes place to improve their undersea diving and salvage skills.

Physical Requirements

The job of a navy diver is physically challenging. Besides being in top physical condition, young people who wish to become navy divers must have normal color vision and have uncorrected vision that is no worse than 20/200 and correctable to 20/25. Candidates must also be thirty years of age or younger. Divers must pass a physical screening test that requires a 500-yard (457 m) swim (sidestroke or breaststroke) in twelve minutes or less; forty-two or more push-ups in two minutes; fifty or more sit-ups in two minutes; six or more dead-hang pull-ups in two minutes; and run 1.5 miles (2 km) in twelve minutes, thirty seconds or faster.

Volunteer Work and Internships

Students interested in a career as a navy diver can learn about navy life by participating in the Junior Reserve Officers' Training Corps

(JROTC) in high school. Participation in the JROTC prepares students physically for basic training. JROTC members also participate in military drills and visit military bases to learn more about life in the armed services.

In addition, students can learn more about a diving career by interning in a civilian company or by shadowing an adult who has a job in this field. Many diving companies offer internships to certified scuba divers who are interested in diving careers.

Skills and Personality

Navy divers should be comfortable working in the water and have excellent swimming skills. They should also have no aversion to being confined in close spaces. According to Paul Canen, the master chief explosive ordnance disposal officer in charge at the Great Lakes training center, one of the hardest things to teach candidates is how to be comfortable in the water. In an article for the Navy magazine *All Hands*, he explains, "Being able to do the task you're having to do even though everything is happening around you in the water and you're gasping for breath and you're having to kick and still being able to work—it's hard to teach that and it's really hard to test for that before you get someplace like here." Navy divers need to be able to work efficiently and calmly, under pressure and in changeable and sometimes poor underwater conditions. They must be able to work independently but also as part of a team.

On the Job

Working Conditions

The navy diver motto is We Dive the World Over. Divers can be assigned anywhere around the globe. The working environment varies according to the water conditions and can sometimes be dangerous. Some assignments may be in cold, muddy water with little visibility. Other assignments may take place in warm, clear, tropical waters.

In the summer of 2015, a navy diving team worked to salvage a Civil War–era ironclad vessel in the Savannah River. The working conditions were challenging, with the water so murky that the divers could not see beyond their hands. At the same time, they had to work against the river's current and avoid jagged pieces of iron and debris all around the site. In an article for the *Las Vegas Review-Journal*, Cody Bumpass, a navy diver first class, says that "if you don't know what you are doing, it could be a little scary."

Earnings

In the Navy, basic pay is based on a service member's rank, also known as rate for enlisted personnel, and years of service. As of January 1, 2015, the base salary for active-duty enlisted service members ranged from $18,564 to $91,020, according to the Navy CyberSpace website. In addition to basic pay, service members may qualify for extra pay or bonuses based on their job assignment or qualifications. For example, they can receive additional pay for foreign, hazardous, or submarine duty. Navy divers are eligible for additional dive pay.

In addition, service members receive other benefits, which can amount to thousands of dollars. Enlisted sailors and officers earn up to thirty days paid vacation or leave each year. Service members receive tax-free allowances for housing and food along with tax-free shopping privileges at military stores. They have the opportunity to travel around the world for free or for a low cost. Other benefits include comprehensive medical and dental care, education benefits, and retirement benefits. The Navy provides all service members with life insurance plans as well.

The Navy also offers enlistment bonuses, which depend on the terms of enlistment, military career choice, and the enlistee's education and qualifications. Enlistment bonuses range from about $2,000 to $40,000. As of July 2015, navy divers can earn an enlistment bonus of $8,000. Reenlistment bonuses are also available for service members in high-demand careers. As of 2015, navy divers may be eligible for reenlistment bonuses of up to $100,000.

Opportunities for Advancement

The Navy provides service members with many opportunities for advancement. Typically, service members receive a raise in pay each time they advance in grade or rank. Sailors generally enlist in the Navy in pay grade E-1, or seaman recruit. They may advance as high as E-9, master chief petty officer.

Promotion for enlisted service members depends on several factors, including performance evaluation marks and proficiency exam scores. Enlisted service members receive regular performance evaluations and must receive a minimum score to be eligible for a promotion. Sailors who demonstrate a record of excellent performance and effective leadership are more likely to be promoted.

Although the Navy does not require divers to hold special licenses or certifications, certifications are important for diving careers and may make service members eligible for promotions. There are several navy-funded certifications available for navy divers, including the advanced open-water diver, air diving supervisor, and life-support technician certifications. In addition, the specialized training that navy divers receive can help them obtain civilian certifications.

The Navy also offers several paths for enlisted members who wish to be commissioned as navy officers. Enlisted members who have already earned a bachelor's degree in college can apply for Officer Candidate School. If they do not have a degree, the Navy offers enlisted members the opportunity to attend college full time and earn a bachelor's degree and then receive a commission. Divers who complete navy training courses may be eligible to earn college credit hours toward a bachelor's or associate degree through the American Council on Education. A promotion to commissioned officer often results in a significant pay raise.

What Is the Future Outlook for Navy Divers?

The United States currently spends a significant amount of its overall budget on national defense. The total number of active-duty and reserve personnel in the Navy is expected to remain about the same for the next several years. As divers leave the Navy or move on to other military careers, the Navy will need to fill these open positions. As a result, new recruits for this field are constantly needed. Currently, advancement opportunities for navy divers are at an all-time high, and the outlook for future growth of this career is very good. However, successfully completing navy diver training is very difficult, with only about seventy-five trainees annually becoming navy divers.

What Are Employment Prospects in the Civilian World?

After leaving the military, navy divers are qualified to work in several civilian careers. Earning civilian certifications as a navy diver can help service members find employment after leaving the military. Their specialized training, expertise, and security clearance allows them to work in jobs with the federal government, including jobs on government-owned ships and those involving the preparation of nautical and marine charts and other information for government agencies. In addition, they may work as civilians as commercial divers, explosives workers, ordnance handling experts, maintenance and repair workers, motorboat operators, welders, cutters, and welder fitters.

JAG Lawyer

What Does a JAG Lawyer Do?

JAG (judge advocate general) lawyers help sailors and the Navy navigate and conduct military operations in an increasingly complex legal and regulatory environment. Based throughout the world on ships and shore, JAG lawyers do work that is critical to the success of military operations worldwide. The JAG Corps assists the Navy with legal matters for military operations around the world and gives legal advice to navy commanders. Members of the JAG Corps also run the Navy's military justice system—the laws and procedures that military service members must follow. The military justice system deals with many of the same crimes as the civilian criminal justice system, such as murder and assault, but it also includes rules and punishments for military-specific crimes, such as leaving a post without permission and disobeying a superior officer's orders. The JAG Corps also supports navy personnel and their families with a variety of legal assistance services.

Navy JAG lawyers are like civilian lawyers in that they prosecute criminal cases, defend clients in court, prepare wills, negotiate

At a Glance:
JAG Lawyer

Minimum Educational Requirements
Law degree

Personal Qualities
Good communication and analytical skills, interpersonal skills, strong writing skills

Certification and Licensing
Must be a licensed attorney in any US state or territory

Working Conditions
An office environment on a ship or at naval stations around the world

Salary Range
Monthly salary depends on pay grade and years of service

Number of Jobs
More than 800

Future Job Outlook
Good

contracts, assist with divorce and child custody cases, and help military personnel with a variety of other legal needs. The difference is that JAG lawyers primarily work under the jurisdiction of military courts and law. During a court-martial, for instance, some JAG lawyers represent the prosecution while others represent the defense. And when complaints of sexual harassment surface, JAG lawyers investigate these complaints and determine whether action is warranted. JAG lawyers also advise ship commanders about a variety of issues, from how to handle a sexual assault case to whether or not gifts can be accepted on behalf of the Navy.

Lieutenant Commander Christopher Swain, an attorney in the JAG Corps, works in the Navy's admiralty and maritime law division. This division is responsible for handling all contracts, claims, injuries, or offenses that take place on navigable waters, including oceans, lakes, and rivers. They advise the Secretary of the Navy, the Chief of Naval Operations, the Judge Advocate General, and navy fleet commanders on legal matters involving these issues. Swain says that his work in the JAG Corps has given him many invaluable experiences. In a video interview on the *US Navy JAG Corps* blog, he explains,

> I think the best thing about being a judge advocate . . . is the amount of incredible experiences that we get to do right off the bat. In my first three years as a JAG, I prosecuted court-martial, I served in Iraq as an individual augmentee overseas [a temporary duty assignment to a unit], and I began a carrier tour and served a couple of years onboard a carrier overseas giving operational law advice to the commander. I think that breadth of experience that we get right off the bat is amazing.

How Do You Become a JAG lawyer?

Education

All navy JAG lawyers are commissioned officers. They are required to have a minimum of a bachelor's degree from an accredited college or university. In addition, they either have to be a licensed attorney or be attending law school. To prepare for a career as a JAG lawyer, high school and college students should take classes that develop skills in writing, analysis, critical thinking, and research. Classes in English, history, civics, and government are all beneficial. Participation on a debate team also provides useful skills for anyone contemplating a career in law.

There are three paths to becoming a navy JAG lawyer. The most common way is through the Student Program. In this program, law students apply to the navy JAG Corps after they finish their first year of law school. If selected, they are commissioned as officers into the inactive navy reserve until they graduate from law school. Alternately, licensed attorneys can be directly appointed to the JAG Corps as lieutenants. For current navy officers who do not have a law degree, the Law Education Program allows them to enter law school, earn a law degree, and then serve as a judge advocate.

Officers in the JAG Corps do not undergo traditional basic training. After acceptance into the JAG Corps and taking the bar exam, service members attend Officer Development School (ODS) in Newport, Rhode Island. ODS is the first step in navy JAG Corps training. Here, JAG lawyers spend five weeks learning about the customs and traditions of naval service. They also learn the basic principles of shipboard navigation; damage control, such as firefighting; flooding measures; and first aid, naval administration, and disciplinary procedures. JAG lawyers in ODS also participate in physical fitness training.

After finishing ODS and passing the bar exam, navy judge advocates attend further training at the Basic Lawyer Course at Naval Justice School in Newport. Over a ten-week period, judge advocates learn civil and military law and military trial procedures. They learn methods of obtaining evidence and receive intensive trial advocacy training. After successfully completing this course, they are certified for service as a navy judge advocate and report for their first duty station.

Certification and Licensing

Navy JAG lawyers must be graduates of accredited law schools and licensed attorneys in any US state or territory.

Volunteer Work and Internships

Interested law students who want to gain experience and learn more about being a navy judge advocate can apply for unpaid JAG Corps internships. Interns are assigned to a legal office. They gain experience in areas such as military justice, legal assistance, and advising military commanders and their staffs.

Students who are interested in becoming a JAG lawyer may also seek volunteer positions with the Legal Aid Society. This nonprofit organization provides free legal information, advice, and representation to people who cannot afford to hire a lawyer. Volunteers assist with legal research, special projects, administrative tasks, and computer services.

Physical Requirements, Skills, and Personality

All JAG Corps members must be US citizens of good moral character. They must be younger than forty-two years old at the time they begin active duty and must be able to meet the physical requirements for a navy commission.

Successful navy judge advocates have several personal characteristics in common. They have a deep commitment to public service and strong leadership skills. Communication skills, both oral and written, are highly desirable. Effective oral communication skills help lawyers make convincing arguments in the courtroom. Writing and reading skills help them prepare and analyze a variety of legal documents.

The ability to think critically and analytically is also important for people considering a career as a navy judge advocate. They should be able to follow the logic of a legal argument or find trouble areas in their own arguments. Lawyers analyze large amounts of information when preparing a case and then must organize and present it in a clear, logical manner so that others can understand it.

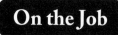

On the Job

Working Conditions

Navy judge advocates generally work in an office environment, either on a ship at sea or at naval bases or stations across the United States and overseas.

Earnings

In the Navy, basic pay is based on a service member's rank and years of service. As of January 1, 2015, the base salary for active-duty officers ranged from $35,208 to $237,156, according to the Navy CyberSpace website. In addition to basic pay, service members may qualify for extra pay or bonuses based on their job assignment or qualifications. For example, they can receive additional pay for foreign, hazardous, or submarine duty.

In addition, service members receive other benefits, which can amount to thousands of dollars. Naval officers earn up to thirty days paid vacation or leave each year, along with ten paid federal holidays, and sick leave for personal medical needs or to care for a family member. Service members receive tax-free allowances for housing and food along with tax-free shopping privileges at military stores. They have the opportunity to travel around the world for free or for a low cost. Other benefits include comprehensive medical and dental care and retirement benefits. Naval officers receive education benefits such as financial assistance for repaying law school loans and funding for continuing education. The Navy also provides all service members with life insurance plans.

The Navy offers enlistment bonuses as well, which depend on the terms of enlistment, military career choice, and the enlistee's education and qualifications. Enlistment bonuses range from about $2,000 to $40,000. After completing their first active-duty assignment, navy JAG Corps officers are eligible for judge advocate continuation pay of up to $60,000, paid in three installments at different career milestones over a ten-year period.

Opportunities for Advancement

The Navy provides service members with many opportunities for advancement. Promotions are generally competitive and based on performance. Typically, service members receive a raise in pay each time they advance in grade.

Navy judge advocates who enter the JAG Corps through direct appointment enter as lieutenants junior grade. They usually are promoted to lieutenant approximately one year after beginning ODS. Judge advocates who enter via the Student Program are commissioned as ensigns. By the time they start the Basic Lawyer Course, they are promoted to lieutenant junior grade and are typically promoted to lieutenant approximately one year later.

Officers in the JAG Corps generally serve approximately six years before becoming eligible for promotion to lieutenant commander. With additional service time, future promotions to commander are possible.

What Is the Future Outlook for JAG Lawyers?

The United States currently spends a significant amount of its overall budget on national defense. The total number of active-duty and reserve personnel in the Navy is expected to remain about the same for the next several years. As judge advocates leave the Navy, their positions will need to be filled. As a result, new recruits for this field are constantly needed. In addition, as the world's legal and regulatory environments become increasingly complex, the Navy will need new legal experts and innovative thinkers.

What Are Employment Prospects in the Civilian World?

While in the Navy, JAG lawyers may be able to obtain civilian certifications from national boards and organizations. These include the estate planning law specialist certification from the National Association of Estate Planners & Council and a board certification in criminal trial advocacy from the National Board of Legal Specialty Certification. Earning these certifications may involve additional navy-funded education, training, and experience and may help a JAG lawyer find civilian work.

After leaving the military, many navy judge advocates work for civilian law firms or companies. Some work as judges in local, state, or federal courts. According to the US Department of Labor, employment of lawyers is expected to grow 10 percent through 2022, which is about the average rate of all occupations. Lawyers will be needed to provide legal services for individuals, business, and all levels of government.

Civil Engineer

What Does a Civil Engineer Do?

Every year the Navy spends millions of dollars on construction projects to support its fleet of ships, aircraft, equipment, and personnel. On each construction project, the Navy's civil engineers take the lead. They supervise and manage construction workers; organize, track, and maintain project budgets and schedules; and ensure that everything proceeds according to plan. When the project is complete, civil engineers approve the final work.

As part of the Navy's Civil Engineer Corps (CEC), civil engineers generally work in one of three areas: construction management, public works, or construction battalions. Airfields, roads, bridges, power plants, and other structures on navy bases are constantly being built or repaired. Civil engineers working in construction management plan, design, and direct the work on these structures. They review designs and prepare, solicit, and award contracts. They closely supervise construction, resolving problems as they arise. If the project uses civilian construction companies and workers, navy civil engineers serve as the primary point of contact between the Navy and the

> ## At a Glance:
> ## Civil Engineer
>
> **Minimum Educational Requirements**
> Bachelor's degree
>
> **Personal Qualities**
> Ability to think logically and solve problems
>
> **Certification and Licensing**
> None
>
> **Working Conditions**
> Indoors and outdoors
>
> **Salary Range**
> Monthly salary depends on pay grade and years of service
>
> **Future Job Outlook**
> Good

civilian contractors. As civil engineer Philip Thompson explains on Careers in the Military, a website sponsored by the US government,

> My most memorable tour was at the naval base at Guantanamo Bay, Cuba, where I directed contractors who were building a water desalinization plant and an addition to the power plant. My greatest satisfaction came from completely remodeling every home on the base. We gutted and remade hot, uncomfortable houses into modern, fully air-conditioned units. It was really appreciated by the Navy and Marine Corps personnel and dependents living at Guantanamo.

Other navy civil engineers serve in public works, operating and maintaining all of the Navy's facilities, including docks and buildings. Like civilian facility managers, civil engineers handle everything at a facility, from power distribution to telecommunications. They supervise and maintain utilities. They schedule and oversee grounds and facilities maintenance. It is their job to make sure that all systems and equipment are working properly, from heating and air-conditioning to transportation.

Some civil engineers serve in one of the Navy's construction battalions. These units are made of highly skilled enlisted sailors, called Seabees, who are trained in construction and defensive combat. Seabees are sent around the world for construction projects and to provide humanitarian relief. These units build roads, airfields, bridges, ports, and any type of building.

How Do You Become a Civil Engineer?

Education

All civil engineers are commissioned officers. They are required to have a minimum of a bachelor's degree from an accredited college or university, preferably in civil, mechanical, or electrical engineering. To prepare for a career as a civil engineer, high school students should take classes in physical education, math, computer science, physics, and engineering. College students should pursue an engineering major, with civil, mechanical, and electrical engineering preferred.

To become a navy civil engineer, candidates must successfully complete officer's training. To become an officer, recruits can enroll in a Reserve Officers' Training Corps (ROTC) program at a civilian college. In this program, they will attend military classes and drills as well as report for midshipman assignments during the summers. Other candidates may choose to attend the US Naval Academy. Admission to the Naval Academy is highly competitive, with only about 10 percent of applicants being accepted each year. These students typically have impeccable academic records and leadership experience. Recruits who already have a bachelor's degree can attend Officer Candidate School, an intensive twelve-week course in military studies held at the naval air station at Newport, Rhode Island.

After being commissioned as an officer, candidates for the CEC attend the basic course at the Civil Engineer Corps Officer School (CECOS) in Port Hueneme, California. During this twelve-week course, officers receive specialized training needed for navy projects.

After graduating from CECOS, new CEC officers are assigned to their first tour of duty. This assignment can be with a construction battalion, a public works division, or in construction contract management. In this assignment, the CEC officer further develops necessary skills through on-the-job training and experience. After their first or second assignment, CEC officers are eligible to earn a navy-funded postgraduate degree in an engineering field at a civilian university or a financial management degree at the Naval Postgraduate School.

Volunteer Work and Internships

Students interested in a career as a civil engineer can learn about navy life by participating in the Junior Reserve Officers' Training Corps (JROTC) in high school and the ROTC in college. Participation in the JROTC and ROTC prepares students physically for basic training. Members also participate in military drills and visit military bases to learn more about life in the armed services. College ROTC members have the opportunity to participate in summer training.

In addition, students can learn more about a civil engineering career by interning with a civilian engineering company or by shadowing an adult who has a job in the industry. Interning is a good way to get on-the-job engineering experience. It can also help students decide whether this field is a good fit for a future career.

Physical Requirements, Skills, and Personality

To be a navy civil engineer, candidates must be US citizens. CEC officers must also be between the ages of nineteen and thirty-four when commissioned, although some waivers may be allowed for older candidates. In addition, candidates must meet the Navy's standards for physical fitness, weight, and/or percentage of body fat at the time of commissioning.

For success as a navy civil engineer, several skills and personality traits are helpful. Good engineers have a strong analytical aptitude and the ability to think logically. They continually examine things, understand how they work, and think about ways to improve them. Good engineers also show great attention to detail. Even the smallest error in a project design or construction plan can cause the entire project to fail, so every detail must be carefully reviewed. Because engineers frequently use complex math calculations through project phases, having good math skills is another important trait for this career. Engineers should also have excellent communication skills and be able to work well with others. On the job, they translate complex technical language into everyday English for nonengineering personnel. The success of a project depends on the engineer's ability to bring together all of the other engineers, contractors, and enlisted personnel on the team.

Because many things can go wrong during a project, civil engineers should be able to think quickly on their feet, troubleshoot, and solve problems. Daily, they rely on a depth of technical knowledge, including computer skills. In addition, as officers, civil engineers should have strong leadership skills and serve as role models for enlisted sailors.

On the Job

Working Conditions

Civil engineers work in a variety of environments. They design projects and review reports in offices at navy bases in the United States and around the world. When assigned to a project, they may work in the field, overseeing construction activities. In addition, civil engineers may be sent to any area of the world to rebuild or develop areas ruined by natural disasters.

Earnings

In the Navy, basic pay is based on a service member's rank and years of service. As of January 1, 2015, the base salary for active-duty officers ranged from $35,208 to $237,156, according to the Navy CyberSpace website. In addition to basic pay, service members may qualify for extra pay or bonuses based on their job assignment or qualifications. For example, they can receive additional pay for foreign, hazardous, or submarine duty. Depending on their duty assignment, civil engineers may be eligible for sea, foreign, or hazardous pay.

In addition, service members receive other benefits, which can amount to thousands of dollars. Naval officers earn up to thirty days paid vacation or leave each year. Service members receive tax-free allowances for housing and food along with tax-free shopping privileges at military stores. They have the opportunity to travel around the world for free or for low cost. Other benefits include comprehensive medical and dental care, education benefits, and retirement benefits. Undergraduate engineering and architecture majors are also eligible for the Civil Engineering Collegiate Program, which offers money to pay for college along with a regular monthly income for up to two years prior to graduation. The Navy also provides all service members with life insurance plans.

The Navy offers enlistment bonuses as well, which depend on the terms of enlistment, military career choice, and the enlistee's education and qualifications. Enlistment bonuses range from about $2,000 to $40,000. Reenlistment bonuses are also available for service members in high-demand careers. Civil engineer officers may be eligible for a $50,000 reenlistment bonus if they sign up for an additional five years of service.

Opportunities for Advancement

The Navy provides service members with many opportunities for advancement. Promotions are generally competitive and based on performance. Civil engineers typically begin their service with the rank of ensign. In many cases, they can expect to be promoted to lieutenant junior grade two years after completing Officer Candidate School and to lieutenant two years later. Service members typically receive a raise in pay each time they advance in grade. In addition, all CEC officers are expected to pursue professional licensure. Getting a professional license is a requirement for senior CEC officers to receive a promotion.

As civil engineers advance, they plan and manage larger projects, lead other engineers, and command combat engineering battalions of hundreds of enlisted personnel. Senior CEC officers are responsible for directing all civil engineering operations at a military base, advising base commanders on engineering matters, and overseeing major engineering projects.

What Is the Future Outlook for Civil Engineers?

The United States currently spends a significant amount of its overall budget on national defense. The total number of active-duty and reserve personnel in the Navy is expected to remain about the same for the next several years. As civil engineers leave the Navy or move on to other military careers, the Navy will need to fill these open positions. As a result, new recruits for this field are constantly needed. In addition, as new global conflicts and threats emerge, there may be an additional demand for military personnel, including civil engineers.

What Are Employment Prospects in the Civilian World?

With their navy training and experience, many CEC engineers are able to obtain civilian certifications and licenses from national boards and organizations. Earning these certifications and licenses can help civil engineers find civilian employment after leaving the Navy. Many civil engineers find jobs with civilian engineering firms, construction companies, and government agencies. Others work for public utilities, railroads, and manufacturing companies. According to the US Department of Labor's *Occupational Outlook Handbook*, jobs for civil engineers are projected to grow 20 percent through 2022, faster than the average rate for all occupations. As the country's infrastructure ages, civil engineers are needed to manage repair and rebuilding projects for structures such as bridges, roads, dams, water systems, and waste treatment plants. In addition, civil engineers are needed to work on renewable energy projects.

Hospital Corpsman

What Does a Hospital Corpsman Do?

At the center of navy medicine, hospital corpsmen provide treatment for thousands of sailors and their families. They provide routine, preventive, and emergency care for sailors around the world. They also provide patient education ranging from basic health and wellness programs to battlefield first-aid training. On ships and in the field, hospital corpsmen monitor environmental sanitation programs and supervise air, water, food, and residence standards.

Hospital corpsmen also serve on the battlefield. Those assigned to a Marine Corps unit, a separate service branch of the US military overseen by the Department of the Navy, work as battlefield medics to save the lives of injured marines. They deploy on search-and-rescue missions and risk their lives to safely carry the wounded out of the line of fire.

In a typical day, hospital corpsmen assist navy doctors, nurses, and dentists, who are all commissioned officers, caring for patients. They run clinical laboratory tests and operate sophisticated laboratory equipment. Others fill prescriptions and maintain pharmacy

At a Glance:
Hospital Corpsman

Minimum Educational Requirements
High school diploma or equivalent

Personal Qualities
Good interpersonal and communication skills, writing and math ability, manual dexterity, good memory

Certification and Licensing
None

Working Conditions
In hospitals or clinics aboard ships and submarines or at land-based stations in the field or on bases

Salary Range
Monthly salary depends on pay grade and years of service

Future Job Outlook
Good

supplies. They work in the operating room as technicians or surgical assistants for general and specialized surgeries. Some corpsmen maintain and repair medical equipment such as kidney dialysis machines, radiation monitors, hearing and vision testing machines, heart and lung test machines, and ultrasound and computed tomography equipment. As part of their administrative responsibilities, hospital corpsmen order medical supplies and update patient records and reports.

Corpsmen can specialize in different areas of medicine. They can work, for example, as biomedical equipment technicians, medical laboratory technicians, dental assistants and hygienists, and field medical service technicians. Those who specialize in dentistry serve as dental assistants, helping with dental procedures and preventive dentistry. They construct dental crowns and bridges or take dental X-rays. Some make and fit artificial teeth, and others repair dental equipment.

Petty Officer Third Class Maria Arvelo enlisted in the Navy at the age of eighteen and chose to become a hospital corpsman. After training, Arvelo was assigned to her first duty station at the National Naval Medical Center in Bethesda, Maryland (known today as the Walter Reed National Military Medical Center). She worked in the emergency room (ER), wrapping broken ankles and monitoring the fevers of sick patients. After her ER duties, Arvelo became the receptionist of a clinic in the cardiology department. She also learned to work in the clinic, pricking patients' fingers to test blood-clotting ability. Today she is assigned to the US Naval Hospital in Rota, Spain, where she works at the radiology department's front desk. She says that her experiences as a hospital corpsman have given her many opportunities, and she hopes to use them to become a nurse one day.

How Do You Become a Hospital Corpsman?

Education

Hospital corpsmen are enlisted sailors. As such, they are required to have a high school diploma. To prepare for this career, high school students should take classes in math, science, physical education, nutrition, and, if available, medical pathway courses. Taking classes in CPR, first aid, and automated external defibrillator use like those

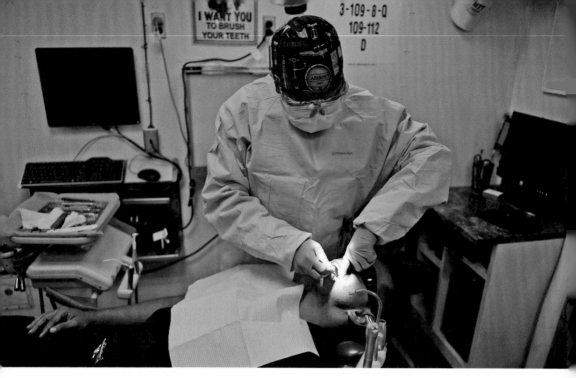

A US Navy hospital corpsman performs a routine cleaning in the dental office aboard the USS Blue Ridge. *Hospital corpsmen handle both routine and emergency medical and dental care for navy and Marine Corps personnel.*

taught by the Red Cross are also good preparation for a career as a hospital corpsman.

Upon joining the Navy, recruits complete an initial seven- to nine-week basic training, called recruit training or boot camp. Recruit training includes instruction in navy skills and protocols. It includes weapons training, team building, and strenuous physical exercise to improve a recruit's strength and endurance.

After recruit training, recruits receive specific training at the Naval Hospital Corps School at Fort Sam Houston, Texas, to prepare for careers as corpsmen. This training lasts for approximately nineteen weeks and develops the working knowledge the sailors will need for their first assignments on a ship or at a base. Training includes classroom lectures as well as hands-on instruction with medical equipment. Recruits learn the basic principles and techniques for patient care and first-aid procedures. They study a variety of subjects, including anatomy, physiology, and emergency medicine.

After this schooling, hospital corpsmen are assigned to their first duty either at a navy medical treatment facility or aboard a navy vessel.

There they receive further experience and training on the job. After their first duty assignment, hospital corpsmen are eligible to take specialized advanced training courses and earn additional certifications.

Physical Requirements

Working as a hospital corpsman can be physically demanding, as they have to lift and carry patients and medical equipment. Therefore, corpsmen should have the physical strength and stamina to handle these tasks. Corpsmen cannot have a history of drug abuse or a record of criminal offenses involving alcohol or drugs. Additionally, corpsmen who wish to work as a dental assistant must have normal color perception.

Volunteer Work and Internships

Students interested in a career as a hospital corpsman can learn about navy life by participating in the Junior Reserve Officers' Training Corps (JROTC) in high school. Participation in the JROTC prepares students physically for basic training. JROTC members also participate in military drills and visit military bases to learn more about life in the armed services.

In addition, students can learn more about a hospital corpsman career by interning or volunteering at a civilian hospital or medical clinic or by shadowing an adult who has a job in the medical field. Through these experiences, they can learn more about working in a hospital setting and the day-to-day responsibilities of medical personnel.

Skills and Personality

Hospital corpsmen should enjoy working with people and have excellent interpersonal skills as they will be interacting with patients and other medical staff on a regular basis. Having a caring bedside demeanor can help make patients feel more comfortable. Hospital corpsmen often have to communicate information about a patient's condition or explain discharge instructions. To be effective, they should be able to speak and write well and communicate clearly. Other important skills for this career include the ability to perform detailed and repetitive work and keep accurate records.

Working Conditions

Hospital corpsmen typically work indoors at hospitals or clinics with other medical staff. Some corpsmen work aboard ships and submarines as medics or with special operations units such as the Navy SEALs or Seabee units. While they often work as part of a team, some may work individually at times.

Hospital corpsmen also can work on the front lines in a war zone. Petty Officer Second Class Michael Soto is a twenty-four-year-old navy hospital corpsman who was deployed with a Marine Corps platoon to Afghanistan in 2011. While there, he treated wounded soldiers, dealing with gunshot wounds, fractures, and amputations. In an article published by Cook County Health and Hospitals System, Soto explained what it was like on the battlefield. "You're going 100 mph, just kinda doing the best you can," Soto said. "You don't know if another guy is going to get injured, so you're patching up one guy really quick, just to hurry up because something might happen to another guy." Often, Soto had to work alone to treat injured soldiers. He described the experience: "Combat is, like, 'OK, here's your med bag, go take care of some Marines.' You don't have a physician, you don't have a nurse next to you. You're it."

Earnings

In the Navy, basic pay is based on a service member's rank, also known as rate for enlisted personnel, and years of service. As of January 1, 2015, the base salary for active-duty enlisted service members ranged from $18,564 to $91,020, according to the Navy CyberSpace website. In addition to basic pay, service members may qualify for extra pay or bonuses based on their job assignment or qualifications. For example, they can receive additional pay for foreign, hazardous, or submarine duty.

In addition, service members receive other benefits, which can amount to thousands of dollars. Enlisted sailors and officers earn up to thirty days paid vacation or leave each year. Service members receive tax-free allowances for housing and food along with tax-free shopping privileges at military stores. They have the opportunity to travel around the world for free or for a low cost. Other benefits include comprehensive medical and dental care, education benefits, and retirement benefits. The Navy also provides all service members with life insurance plans.

The Navy offers enlistment bonuses as well, which depend on the terms of enlistment, military career choice, and the enlistee's education and qualifications. Enlistment bonuses range from about $2,000 to $40,000. Reenlistment bonuses are also available for service members in high-demand careers. Hospital corpsmen may be eligible for a reenlistment bonus of up to $60,000.

Opportunities for Advancement

The Navy provides service members with many opportunities for advancement. Typically, service members receive a raise in pay each time they advance in grade or rank. Sailors generally enlist in the Navy in pay grade E-1, or seaman recruit. They may advance as high as E-9, master chief petty officer.

Promotion for enlisted service members depends on several factors, including performance evaluation marks and proficiency exam scores. Enlisted service members receive regular performance evaluations and must receive a minimum score to be eligible for a promotion. In addition, enlisted sailors from pay grade E-3 to E-6 must do well on promotion exams in order to earn a promotion to a higher rank. These examinations test the sailor for general navy knowledge and career-specific proficiency. Sailors who demonstrate a record of excellent performance and effective leadership are more likely to be promoted.

Although the Navy does not require hospital corpsmen to hold special licenses or certifications, certifications are important to medical careers and promotions. There are many navy-funded civilian certifications available for hospital corpsmen from a number of national boards and organizations. For example, corpsmen can earn the EKG (electrocardiogram) technician certification from the National Healthcareer Association and the safety technician certification from the World Safety Council. Earning these certifications can make hospital corpsmen eligible for promotions as well as help them find civilian employment after leaving the military.

The Navy also offers several paths for enlisted members who wish to be commissioned as navy officers. Enlisted members who have already earned a bachelor's degree in college can apply for Officer Candidate School. If they do not have a degree, the Navy offers enlisted members the opportunity to attend college full time and earn a bachelor's degree and then receive a commission. In addition, hospital corpsmen who complete navy medical training may be eligible to earn college credit hours toward a bachelor's or associate degree through the American Council on Education. A promotion to commissioned officer often results in a significant pay raise.

What Is the Future Outlook for Hospital Corpsmen?

The United States currently spends a significant amount of its overall budget on national defense. The total number of active-duty and reserve personnel in the Navy is expected to remain about the same for the next several years. As corpsmen leave the Navy or move on to other military careers, the Navy will need to fill these open positions. As a result, new recruits for this field are constantly needed. In addition, as new global conflicts and threats emerge, there may be an additional demand for military personnel, including hospital corpsmen.

What Are Employment Prospects in the Civilian World?

After leaving the military, hospital corpsmen are qualified to work in a wide range of medical careers. Their specialized training and experience allow them to work for the federal government or civilian hospitals and clinics. They can work as medical and physician assistants, emergency medical technicians and paramedics, orderlies, nursing assistants, and anesthesiology assistants. They are also well prepared for education and training to become doctors and nurses. According to the US Department of Labor's *Occupational Outlook Handbook*, jobs for physician assistants are projected to grow 38 percent through 2022, much faster than the average for all occupations.

Nuclear Surface Warfare Officer

What Does a Nuclear Surface Warfare Officer Do?

The Navy's nuclear-powered aircraft carriers are some of the world's most technologically advanced ships. Instead of burning fossil fuel for power, these ships use an onboard nuclear reactor to generate power for propulsion and shipboard equipment. Using nuclear power eliminates the need for the ships to refuel during a long operation at sea.

Nuclear surface warfare officers (NSWOs) make sure that these complex ships run safely, smoothly, and effectively for all naval missions. On the America's Navy YouTube channel, Lieutenant Monika Coxe, an NSWO, explains her responsibilities onboard her vessel: "As a surface warfare officer, you're ultimately responsible for all the lives on board your ship. . . . You're driving the ship, making sure the ship gets to the location that it needs to, making sure that you're avoiding anything that could be hazardous to the ship."

At a Glance:
Nuclear Surface Warfare Officer

Minimum Educational Requirements
Bachelor's degree

Personal Qualities
Ability to solve problems and think clearly under pressure

Certification and Licensing
None

Working Conditions
On ships and submarines and at shore stations

Salary Range
Monthly salary depends on pay grade and years of service

Future Job Outlook
Good

NSWOs manage a ship's operations so that nothing interferes with the crew's mission. They oversee the day-to-day operations aboard nuclear-powered aircraft carriers in the Navy's fleet. They manage everything from shipboard vertical launch systems and communications to advanced technology for battle and ship defense. In addition, these officers provide support to navy special forces and missions. At sea, NSWOs command a division of sailors aboard a navy ship. The division is responsible for a certain part of the ship's equipment or operations, such as a specific electronic system or weapon. NSWOs are responsible for making sure that the sailors in their division maintain and operate the ship's systems safely and efficiently. Lieutenant Chris Zundel is an NSWO who oversees the nuclear propulsion system on the aircraft carrier *Nimitz*. In a navy nuclear propulsion program video, he explains what he does on the job: "My daily routine is to basically stand watch and run a division that maintains a lot of the equipment, the supports, the reactor aboard the USS *Nimitz*. Making sure that any maintenance that goes on gets done correctly and safely. And we're also making sure that the ship is continuing to make water, make electricity, and push the ship through the water."

How Do You Become a Nuclear Surface Warfare Officer?

Education

All NSWOs are commissioned officers. They are required to have a minimum of a bachelor's degree from an accredited college or university, preferably with a major in mathematics, engineering, physics, chemistry, or other technical field. To prepare for a career as an NSWO, high school students should take classes in physical education, math, computer science, physics, chemistry, and engineering. College students can choose any major, although majors in math, chemistry, physics, or another technical field are preferred.

NSWOs must successfully complete officer's training. To become an officer, recruits can enroll in a Reserve Officers' Training Corps (ROTC) program at a civilian college. In this program, they will attend military classes and drills as well as report for midshipman assignments during the summer. Other candidates may choose to attend the US Naval Academy. Admission to the Naval Academy is highly competitive, with only about 10 percent of applicants being accepted each year. These students typically have impeccable academic records, leadership experience, and participate in varsity sports. Recruits who already have a bachelor's degree can attend Officer Candidate School, an intensive twelve-week course in military studies held at the naval air station at Newport, Rhode Island.

Newly commissioned officers who wish to become NSWOs are assigned to their first sea tour as a division officer on a conventional ship. In this assignment, they command a team of enlisted sailors and are responsible for a specific operation or system on the ship. On this assignment, officers work toward earning a surface warfare qualification.

After the first sea tour, candidates attend Nuclear Power School (NPS). During this six-month course in Charleston, South Carolina, they study a variety of science and technology subjects, including thermodynamics and reactor dynamics. This course gives officers the basic knowledge they need to understand nuclear propulsion.

After this course, officers enter the Nuclear Power Training Unit, a six-month course known as Prototype. It includes hands-on training with several nuclear reactor prototypes. The officers apply the concepts that they learned at NPS as they study the systems and components of a nuclear propulsion plant and work with a full-scale operating plant. Upon completion of this training, an officer is qualified as an engineering officer of the watch.

Having proven their abilities on a conventional ship and in nuclear training, the next step in NSWO training is assignment on a second sea tour. This time, officers are assigned to a nuclear-powered aircraft carrier and serve as a division officer in the carrier's engineering plant.

Volunteer Work and Internships

Students interested in a career as an NSWO can learn about navy life by participating in the Junior Reserve Officers' Training Corps (JROTC) in high school and the ROTC in college. Participation in the JROTC and ROTC prepares students physically for basic training. Members also participate in military drills and visit military bases to learn more about life in the armed services. College ROTC members also have the opportunity to participate in summer training.

Qualified college students can take a two-day VIP trip to experience the world of a surface warfare officer. On the trip, students tour the flight deck of an aircraft carrier and walk through a submarine. They also have the opportunity to talk to current NSWOs and ask questions about their job. This experience can help students learn firsthand about an NSWO career.

Physical Requirements, Skills, and Personality

To be an NSWO, candidates must be US citizens. Officers must also be between the ages of nineteen and twenty-nine when commissioned, although some waivers may be allowed for candidates up to thirty-one years old. In addition, candidates must meet the Navy's standards for physical fitness, weight, and/or percentage of body fat at the time of commissioning.

Because many things can go wrong during a mission, NSWOs should be able to think quickly on their feet, troubleshoot, and solve problems. They must be able to keep calm during times of intense stress and be able to make quick, logical decisions. In addition, as officers, NSWOs should have strong leadership skills. They are responsible for the safety and protection of their crew, and they serve as role models for enlisted navy service members.

On the Job

Working Conditions

NSWOs work in a variety of environments, from academic settings on shore to training on prototype units or serving on conventional ships and nuclear-powered aircraft carriers around the world. Deployments at sea can last for several months at a time.

Earnings

In the Navy, basic pay is based on a service member's rank and years of service. As of January 1, 2015, the base salary for active-duty officers ranged from \$35,208 to \$237,156, according to the Navy CyberSpace website. In addition to basic pay, service members may qualify for extra pay or bonuses based on their job assignment or qualifications. For example, they can receive additional pay for foreign, hazardous, or submarine duty.

In addition, service members receive other benefits, which can amount to thousands of dollars. Naval officers earn up to thirty days paid vacation or leave each year. Service members receive tax-free allowances for housing and food along with tax-free shopping privileges at military stores. They have the opportunity to travel around the world for free or for low cost. Other benefits include comprehensive medical and dental care, education benefits, and retirement benefits. The Navy also provides all service members with life insurance plans.

The Navy offers enlistment bonuses as well, which depend on the terms of enlistment, military career choice, and the enlistee's education and qualifications. Enlistment bonuses range from about \$2,000 to \$40,000. Reenlistment bonuses are also available for service members in high-demand careers. NSWOs are eligible for continuation pay up to \$50,000 if they choose to remain on active duty after completing their initial tour.

Opportunities for Advancement

The Navy provides service members with many opportunities for advancement. Promotions are generally competitive and based on performance. Typically, service members receive a raise in pay each time they advance in grade. As NSWOs advance, they can be promoted on future sea tours and put in command of a ship's department, commanding all of the divisions that fall into that department, such as engineering, combat systems, or operations. NSWOs generally serve two sea tours of eighteen months each before serving in a shore-duty role on a major command's staff or at a military postgraduate school. Senior NSWOs can serve as the commanding officer of a ship.

What Is the Future Outlook for Nuclear Surface Warfare Officers?

The United States currently spends a significant amount of its overall budget on national defense. The total number of active-duty and reserve personnel in the Navy is expected to remain about the same for the next several years. As surface warfare officers leave the Navy or move on to other military careers, the Navy will need to fill these open positions. As a result, new recruits for this field are constantly needed. In addition, as new global conflicts and threats emerge, there may be an additional demand for military personnel, including NSWOs.

What Are Employment Prospects in the Civilian World?

With their navy training and experience, NSWOs may be able to obtain civilian certifications and licenses from national boards and organizations. Earning these certifications and licenses can help with the transition to civilian employment. Navy-trained nuclear power specialists are highly sought after in the nuclear power industry, taking jobs with nuclear power plants and energy companies. Other NSWOs use their technical skills to work for civilian engineering companies. Some work as oceanographers or as information technologists on research submarines and ships. Others work as ship pilots, boat captains, radio operators, and ship engineers. NSWOs can also use their leadership skills to become management analysts, managers, and human resource executives at civilian companies.

Cryptologic Technician

Gathering top secret intelligence is a critical part of keeping the United States secure. Working under the oversight of information warfare officers or cyberwarfare engineers, the Navy's cryptologic technicians use their skills and the latest technology to collect, decode, and translate intelligence information, such as encrypted electronic communications. They also jam the enemy's radar signals, preventing them from relaying information or using radar-equipped weapons. Cryptologic technicians translate communications and other information transmitted in foreign languages. They also maintain the high-tech equipment that the Navy uses to gather intelligence and defend these networks from attack. Vice Admiral Michael Rogers, head of the Navy's Fleet Cyber Forces, says that it is common to find one hundred probes looking to infiltrate navy networks in a single twenty-four-hour period.

At a Glance:

Cryptologic Technician

Minimum Educational Requirements

High school diploma or equivalent

Personal Qualities

Excellent electronics and technology skills, ability to perform highly detailed work, trustworthy

Certification and Licensing

Top secret/sensitive compartmented information security clearances

Working Conditions

On ships, submarines, or aircraft or at land-based shore stations in the United States or overseas

Salary Range

Monthly salary depends on pay grade and years of service

Future Job Outlook

Good

US Navy cryptologic technicians conduct a system diagnostic test aboard the amphibious dock landing ship USS Ashland. *Cryptologic technicians design security procedures and monitor traffic on military computer servers and networks.*

Some are simply e-mail spam, but others are looking for weak points in the Navy's networks to enter and steal data. As Rogers explains on NavyTimes.com, "You will see IP [Internet protocol] addresses beaconing out to others, and that is an immediate red flare for us. 'OK, what is the system doing talking to the outside world? This is not an address we would traditionally associate with normal network operations.'" To protect against these probes and cyberattacks, cryptologic technicians design security procedures and monitor traffic on military computer servers and networks.

Cryptologic technicians are an important part of the Navy's Information Dominance Corps (IDC). Created in 2009, this group includes enlisted sailors, officers, and civilian professionals who specialize in fields such as information technology, cryptology, and intelligence. They work together to develop and defend the Navy's intelligence, networks, and systems and to ensure the Navy's technological superiority. Within the IDC, cryptologic technicians gather information about the enemy's operations, along with critical information about the environment and local conditions that will help sailors during wartime conflicts.

Navy cryptologic technicians usually have a specialty. Interpretive cryptologic technicians, for instance, are language experts. Their fluency in other languages allows them to interpret and translate foreign communications and information. Other cryptologic technicians have a technical specialty. Experts in radar signals, they operate electronic intelligence-receiving systems, digital recording devices, analysis terminals, and related computer equipment. They run electronic equipment to send high-power jamming signals that fool the enemy's electronic sensors and radar-guided weapons systems. Other cryptologic technicians specialize in maintaining the Navy's sophisticated cryptologic equipment, networks, and systems. Others specialize in intercepting and collecting enemy communication signals, and then analyzing the signals to identify and locate potential threats.

Cryptologic technicians who specialize in networks defend and repair the Navy's communications networks. They monitor, identify, collect, and analyze network information. Terrence Savala, a network cryptologic technician, joined the Navy with an interest in computer systems. During his first few years, he maintained the Navy's networks. Recently, he has moved into the cyberwarfare arena, monitoring network data and searching for any suspicious activity. He says that the skills provided by cryptologic technicians are becoming increasingly important as technology advances and the world becomes more connected online. As he explains in an article on NavyTimes .com, "It's fast-paced—that's the war we're fighting in. It's not pencils and paper; it's not tanks and guns any more. It's bits and pieces and networks going across our country."

How Do You Become a Cryptologic Technician?

Education

Cryptologic technicians are enlisted sailors. As such, they are required to have a high school diploma. To prepare for this career, high school students should take classes in computer and networks technology, computer programming, and math. Those interested in the language specialty should also study foreign languages and cultures. Upon joining the Navy, recruits complete an initial seven- to nine-week basic training, called recruit training or boot camp. Recruit training includes instruction in navy skills and protocols. It includes weapons training, team building, and strenuous physical exercise to improve a recruit's strength and endurance.

After recruit training, recruits receive specific training at either the Center for Information Dominance in Pensacola, Florida, or the Defense Language Institute in Monterey, California, to prepare them for careers as navy cryptologic technicians. This training develops the working knowledge the sailors will need for their first assignments on a ship or at a shore station. Training includes classroom lectures as well as hands-on instruction with equipment. It includes extensive technical preparation in computer systems, network configuration, communication techniques and platforms, cryptographic equipment operations, and security policies and procedures. Recruits pursuing a language specialty receive comprehensive foreign language instruction.

Some cryptologic technicians attend advanced classes at the Center for Information Dominance or the Defense Language Institute to receive additional training specific to their specialty. Interpretive recruits receive additional language training, along with technical training. Network recruits practice detecting, reacting, and recovering from attacks on computers and computer networks. Technical recruits learn the operation of digital collection devices and radar analysis equipment.

Certification and Licensing

No special certification or licensing is required to be a cryptologic technician. Because they handle classified information and communications, cryptologic technicians must have top secret/sensitive compartmented information security clearances. In order to gain these security clearances, a candidate must be a US citizen and not have a police record. He or she must also pass a background investigation, with a reinvestigation every five years. Those who have been convicted of drug charges are typically ineligible for this career.

Volunteer Work and Internships

Students interested in a career as a cryptologic technician can learn about navy life by participating in the Junior Reserve Officers' Training Corps (JROTC) in high school. Participation in the JROTC prepares students physically for basic training. JROTC members also participate in military drills and visit military bases to learn more about life in the armed services.

In addition, students can learn more about computer and networking careers by interning in a civilian company's information systems department or by shadowing an adult who has a job in this field. Companies in a variety of industries utilize technology and computer systems and employ professionals to maintain and operate these systems.

Physical Requirements, Skills, and Personality

To become a cryptologic technician, candidates must meet the Navy's standards for physical fitness, weight, and/or percentage of body fat. They must also have normal hearing. For technical and maintenance specialties, candidates must have normal color perception.

Cryptologic technicians should enjoy working with and have a good understanding of computers, electrical and mechanical systems, satellite systems, and other high-tech equipment. They should have the ability to understand and apply math concepts. They should also be able to speak and write well and communicate effectively. Cryptologic technicians need to be able to think creatively, solve problems, and adapt to changing conditions. "You have got to be willing to think out of the box in a nonlinear way. You have got to be flexible and adaptable," explains Rogers. Other important skills for this career include having good moral character, a good memory, curiosity, and the ability to perform detailed work and keep accurate records.

Cryptologic technicians often work as part of a team. Therefore, the ability to work well with others is an important trait for people considering this career. Also, cryptologic technicians should be able to take and follow orders from superior officers. When stress levels are high during a military operation, they should be able to operate calmly and efficiently.

On the Job

Working Conditions

Cryptologic technicians can work aboard ships, submarines, naval aircraft, or at shore stations in the United States or overseas. Their work stations are generally located in clean, air-conditioned offices, computers rooms, or labs with electronic equipment. Joshua Beemer, an interpretive cryptologic technician, is stationed at the Navy Information Operations Command at Fort Gordon, Georgia. From his office, he monitors pirates, hijacked ships, and maritime crime around the world. For Beemer and other cryptologic technicians, sometimes the hours can be long and the workload can quickly increase.

Cryptologic technicians sometimes serve with overseas units during a conflict. Before his assignment at Fort Gordon, Beemer spent eight months with an army unit at Bagram Airfield in Afghanistan. There, he provided tactical war fighters with time-sensitive intelligence on improvised explosive device placement and other threats. He also worked in detention facilities, making sure that America and its allies had gathered enough intelligence to keep insurgents locked up and held for trial.

Earnings

In the Navy, basic pay is based on a service member's rank, also known as rate for enlisted personnel, and years of service. As of January 1, 2015, the base salary for active-duty enlisted service members ranged from $18,564 to $91,020, according to the Navy CyberSpace website. Service members also may qualify for extra pay or bonuses based on their job assignment or qualifications. For example, they can receive additional pay for foreign, hazardous, or submarine duty.

In addition, service members receive other benefits, which can amount to thousands of dollars. These benefits include paid vacation, housing and food allowances, and tax-free shopping privileges at military stores. Other benefits include comprehensive medical and dental care, education benefits, retirement benefits, and life insurance. The Navy offers enlistment bonuses as well, which depend on the terms of enlistment, military career choice, and the enlistee's education and qualifications. Enlistment bonuses range from about $2,000 to $40,000. Reenlistment bonuses are also available for service members in high-demand careers. Cryptologic technicians may be eligible for a reenlistment bonus up to $75,000.

Opportunities for Advancement

The Navy provides service members with many opportunities for advancement. Typically, service members receive a raise in pay each time they advance in grade or rank. Sailors generally enlist in the Navy in pay grade E-1, or seaman recruit. They may advance as high as E-9, master chief petty officer. As cryptologic technicians advance to higher ranks, they take on more supervisory and administrative roles.

Promotion for enlisted service members depends on several factors, including performance evaluation marks and proficiency exam scores. Enlisted service members receive regular performance evaluations and must receive a minimum score to be eligible for a promotion. In addition, enlisted sailors from pay grade E-3 to E-6 must do well on promotion exams in order to earn a promotion to a higher rank. These examinations test the sailor for general navy knowledge and career-specific proficiency. Sailors who demonstrate a record of excellent performance and effective leadership are more likely to be promoted.

Earning certifications can make cryptologic technicians eligible for promotions. There are many navy-funded certifications available, including those in networking, network security, computer forensics, and language skills. Those trained in network specialties can earn certifications in computer hardware and architecture, networking concepts and design, protocol analysis, Windows and Unix programming, and network defense and forensics. In addition, the specialized training that navy cryptologic technicians receive can help them obtain civilian certifications from a number of national boards and organizations.

The Navy also offers several paths for enlisted members who wish to be commissioned as navy officers. Enlisted members who have already earned a bachelor's degree in college can apply for Officer Candidate School. If they do not have a degree, the Navy offers enlisted members the opportunity to attend college full time and earn a bachelor's degree and then receive a commission. In addition, cryptologic technicians who complete navy training in information systems may be eligible to earn college credit hours toward a bachelor's or associate degree through the American Council on Education. A promotion to commissioned officer often results in a significant pay raise.

What Is the Future Outlook for Cryptologic Technicians?

The United States currently spends a significant amount of its over-all budget on national defense. The total number of active-duty and reserve personnel in the Navy is expected to remain about the same for the next several years. As cryptologic technicians leave the Navy or move on to other military careers, the Navy will need to fill these open positions. As a result, new recruits for this field are constantly needed. In addition, as new global conflicts and threats emerge, there may be an additional demand for military personnel, including cryptologic technicians.

What Are Employment Prospects in the Civilian World?

After the military, cryptologic technicians are qualified to work in a wide range of careers. The civilian computer certifications they earn while in the Navy can help them find civilian employment after leaving the military. Their specialized training, expertise, and security clearance may allow them to work in jobs with the federal government, including positions in intelligence and information technology management. In addition, they can work as civilians for a wide range of companies as computer and information systems managers; computer systems analysts; database administrators; network and computer systems administrators; and radio, cellular, and network equipment installers and repairers.

Interview with a Navy Civil Engineer

Alfred Nuzzolo is a navy civil engineer. He has served in the Navy for fifteen years, including one combat tour in Iraq and one in Afghanistan. He is currently serving active duty. He answered questions about his military career by e-mail with the author.

Q: How long have you served in the Navy? Did you serve in any combat tours? If so, how many and where?

A: I have been in the Navy for fifteen years. I served two combat tours, one in An Numaniyah, Iraq, and one in Kandahar, Afghanistan. Fortunately, although it was always a possibility, I was never in active combat.

Q: Why did you join the Navy?

A: I wanted to be in the military probably since middle school, which stemmed from a sense of patriotism and desire to serve my country. I had intended to join the military via one of the service academies, but that did not work out as I planned. I finally came in through a different program while I was attending college as a way to have an income while I was still in school.

Q: Why did you become a civil engineer in the Navy?

A: The program that I came into the Navy through is called the Baccalaureate Degree Completion Program (BDCP). I was attending college pursuing a degree in computer engineering as I had an interest in both math and science and felt such a degree would serve me well. The BDCP was to enter the Civil Engineer Corps upon completion of any engineering degree. I felt it was a way to tie my interests and my desire to serve my country together.

Q: How did you train for this career?

A: The first step was completing an engineering degree. Upon completion, I attended Officer Candidate School, which is one of several ways that a person can become a commissioned officer in the Navy. Since then, the Navy has provided additional training in my field, which has included paying for me to attend graduate school, where I received a master's degree in civil engineering with a concentration in construction.

Q: Can you describe your typical workday?

A: This is difficult to do because we do not really have typical workdays. We have the responsibility of maintaining all the facilities and utilities on a military base along with all related construction and renovation projects and service contracts, such as grounds maintenance, janitorial, and refuse.

Q: What do you like most and least about your job?

A: There are many things I like about my job. First, I really like the people I work with. I have become friends with people from around the United States and around the world. They each bring a different perspective but share a love for their country. I also like the opportunities my family and I have had to travel to different places in the United States and the world, and I do enjoy the fact that things are different from day to day. My least favorite thing about my job is the fiscal (money) constraints. As the budget for the military is cut, it is typically in the facilities and installations where the cuts are most noticed as our country does its best to maintain the ships, planes, and other systems that are used in defense of our country. This always makes our job challenging.

Q: What personal qualities do you find most valuable for this type of work?

A: As a military officer and engineer there are many things that are important/valuable. It is important to be able to lead and to make a decision, but ultimately to realize that it is important to take care of the people that work for and with you. If/when you do this, success in whatever position you find yourself in will follow.

Q: What is the one thing that people might not know about this career?

A: Only about 1 percent of the population has ever served in the military, so that means that what most people know or think they know about the military likely comes from the news or TV shows. I would suggest that neither of these paints a very good picture. In the military as everywhere else, there are bad people that have no business being in the military, but for the most part military personnel are hardworking and dedicated individuals who desire only the best for our country.

Q: What advice do you have for students who might be interested in this career?

A: Try to be involved in a variety of activities throughout your high school years. Good grades are important, but the military and most other corporations are looking for well-rounded individuals who have a wide array of experiences to draw from. Find a mentor or mentors that are doing what you want to do and pick their brains. You will learn a lot about a particular career from people who are doing the work now. AND MOST IMPORTANT. . . have fun. If you get into something that you do not enjoy, life will be miserable.

Find Out More

America's Navy
website: www.navy.com
The official website of the Navy offers information about navy careers, training, and how to join.

Bureau of Labor Statistics
website: www.bls.gov
This website, produced by the US Department of Labor, has information about many different careers, including military careers. Its *Occupational Outlook Handbook* includes career-specific descriptions, pay information, job outlook, and other information.

Careers in the Military
website: www.careersinthemilitary.com
Sponsored by the US Department of Defense, this website provides information about careers in every branch of the US military, including the Navy.

Today's Military
website: www.todaysmilitary.com
Produced by the US Department of Defense, this website has information about each branch of the military and military careers.

USMiltary.com
website: www.usmilitary.com
This website features information about the five branches of the military and the careers in each branch. It also includes information about military testing, basic training, and military news.

US Naval Academy
121 Blake Rd.
Annapolis, MD 21402
phone: (410) 293-1000
website: www.usna.edu/homepage.php
The Naval Academy prepares young men and women to become commissioned officers in the Navy and Marine Corps. The school website provides information about navy careers and training.

Other Jobs in the Navy

Aerospace maintenance duty
officer

Air traffic controller

Aviation boatswain's mate

Aviation electronics technician

Aviation machinist mate

Aviation structural mechanic

Boatswain's mate

Chaplain

Damage controlman

Electrician's mate

Electronic warfare technician

Engineman

Fire control technician

Gunner's mate

Hull technician

Human resources specialist

Intelligence specialist

Logistics specialist

Machinist's mate

Mass communications specialist

Master at arms

Meteorology and oceanography
officer

Missile technician

Musician

Naval flight officer

Naval reactors engineer

Nurse

Physician

Public affairs officer

Serviceman

Sonar technician

Steelworker

Submarine officer

Supply officer

Yeoman

Index

Note: Boldface page numbers indicate illustrations.

active duty, 8
Arvelo, Maria, 53
Aviation Selection Test Battery, 26
aviator. *See* naval aviator

Benfield, Shelly Beck, 5, 8
Bumpass, Cody, 36

civil engineer
  certification/licensing, 45
  educational requirements, 45,
    46–47
  future job outlook, 45, 50
  interview with, 73–75
  prospects for civilian
    employment, 50–51
  role of, 45–46
  salary/earnings, 45, 49–50
  skills/personal qualities, 45, 48
  volunteer work/internships,
    47–48
  working conditions, 45, 48–49
Coll-Dimayo, Marco A., 18
commissioned officers, 7
  paths for enlisted members to
    become, 15
  salary ranges, 6
Coxe, Monika, 59
cryptologic technician, 66
  advancement opportunities,
    71–72
  certification/licensing, 65, 68
  educational requirements, 65,
    67–68
  future job outlook, 65, 72
  prospects for civilian
    employment, 72
  role of, 65–67
  salary/earnings, 65, 70–71
  skills/personal qualities, 65, 69
  volunteer work/internships, 69
  working conditions, 65, 70
culinary specialist, 16, 17
  advancement opportunities,
    21–22
  certification/licensing, 16, 19
  educational requirements, 16,
    18–19
  future job outlook, 16
  number of jobs for, 16
  prospects for civilian
    employment, 23
  salary/earnings, 16, 21
  skills/personal qualities, 16,
    19–20
  volunteer work/internships, 19
  working conditions, 16, 20–21

Department of Labor, US, 44
diver. *See* navy diver

enlisted sailors, 7
  base pay for, 14

salary ranges for, 6
Everage, Coy, 32

Gomez, Israel, 10–11

Haiti, 2010 earthquake in, 5
hospital corpsman
 advancement opportunities,
  57–58
 certification/licensing, 52
 educational requirements, 52,
  53–54
 future job outlook, 52, 58
 physical requirements, 55
 prospects for civilian
  employment, 58
 role of, 52–53
 salary/earnings, 52, 56–57
 skills/personal qualities, 52, 55
 volunteer work/internships, 54
 working conditions, 52, 56
humanitarian missions, 5

Information Dominance Corps
 (IDC), 66–67
information systems technician
 (IST)
 advancement opportunities,
  14–15
 certification/licensing, 9, 12
 educational requirements, 9, 11
 future job outlook, 9
 prospects for civilian
  employment, 15
 role of, 9–11
 salary/earnings, 9, 13–14
 skills/personal qualities, 9, 12–13
 volunteer work/internships, 12
 working conditions, 9, 13

JAG (judge advocate general)
 lawyer
 advancement opportunities,
  43–44
 certification/licensing, 39, 41
 educational requirements, 39,
  40–41
 future job outlook, 39, 44
 number of jobs, 39
 prospects for civilian
  employment, 44
 role of, 39–40
 salary/earnings, 39, 43
 skills/personal qualities, 39, 42
 volunteer work/internships, 42
 working conditions, 39
Jones, Iryll, 33
Junior Reserve Officers' Training
 Corps (JROTC), 28–29, 34–35,
  61–62, 69

Naval Academy, US, 25, 61, 75
naval aviator
 advancement opportunities, 30
 certification/licensing, 24
 educational requirements, 24,
  25–26
 future job outlook, 24
 physical requirements, 27–28
 prospects for civilian
  employment, 30–31
 role of, 24–25
 salary/earnings, 24, 29–30
 skills/personal qualities, 24, 28
 volunteer work/internships,
  28–29
 working conditions, 24, 29
Navy, US
 enlisted vs. officer positions, 7
 history of, 4

requirements/qualifications to join, 5, 7

types of duty in, 8

Navy CyberSpace (website), 21, 29, 36, 43, 49, 56, 63

navy diver
  advancement opportunities, 36–37
  certification/licensing, 32
  educational requirements, 32, 33–34
  future job outlook, 32, 37
  number of jobs for, 32
  physical requirements, 34
  prospects for civilian employment, 38
  salary/earnings, 32, 36
  skills/personal qualities, 32
  volunteer work/internships, 34–35
  working conditions, 32, 35–36

Navy Medicine Live (blog), 5

Nuclear Power School (NPS), 61

nuclear surface warfare officer (NSWO)
  advancement opportunities, 63
  certification/licensing, 59
  educational requirements, 59, 60–61
  future job outlook, 59, 64
  prospects for civilian employment, 64
  role of, 59–60
  salary/earnings, 59, 62–63
  skills/personal qualities, 59, 62
  working conditions, 59, 62

Nuzzolo, Alfred, 73

Occupational Outlook Handbook (US Department of Labor), 23, 31, 51, 58

Officer Development School (ODS), 41

physical requirements
  civil engineer, 42
  cryptologic technician, 69
  culinary specialist, 19–20
  hospital corpsman, 55
  information systems technician, 12–13
  JAG lawyer, 42
  naval aviator, 27–28
  navy diver, 34
  nuclear surface warfare officer, 62

Prototype (training course), 61

reserve duty, 8

Reserve Officers' Training Corps (ROTC), 25, 28–29, 61–62

Rogers, Michael, 65, 66

salaries/pay grades, 7
  enlisted vs. officer, **6**
  See also specific careers

Savala, Terrence, 67

Soto, Michael, 56

Swain, Christopher, 40

Thompson, Philip, 46

Today's Military (website), 25

travel, 8

US Navy JAG Corps (blog), 40

Waddell, James, 25

Zundel, Chris, 60

About the Author

Carla Mooney is the author of many books for young adults and children. She lives in Pittsburgh, Pennsylvania, with her husband and three children.

DISCARDED